THE ELSEWHERE

THE
ELSEWHERE

Poems & Poetics

PHILIP BRADY

BROADSTONE

Library of Congress Control No. 2020945402

ISBN 978-1-937968-73-1

Text Design by Larry W. Moore
Cover Design by Lisa Reynolds
Cover artwork by Robert Carioscia,
used by permission

Broadstone Books
An Imprint of
Broadstone Media LLC
418 Ann Street
Frankfort, KY 40601-1929
BroadstoneBooks.com

In loving memory of Philip & Anne Brady
1918-1994

CONTENTS

INTRODUCTION

from *By Heart: Reflections of a Rust Belt Bard*

Curriculum for a Bardic School

I am a bard. There, I've said it. Embarrassing, like wearing a sign saying "HUMBLE," or announcing you're a secret agent. Still, I have to come clean. Living in this country, in this era, is too trying. In Ireland it was no big deal. You could recite the length of your arm and not be bothered. I once heard a woman in a Donegal pub do the entire Molly Bloom soliloquy impromptu, right down to her knickers, and the two bogmen in the snug never unclenched their pipes. And Africa, teaching in the then province of Shaba in the then nation of Zaire, what with no books anyway and fidgety lightbulbs, reciting poems was just passing on the news, as well as a way to warn off snakes on the walk home. But in the U.S. we leave singing to the pros. When I toss my head back and take flight, I'm seen as a ham, or an autist who might be useful counting cards, or a Lothario, or a compulsive. Then there are the gobshites exclaiming, "How do you remember all that?" And last week a passerby in a business suit slipped me a buck.

I never intended to become a bard, even if I was a fey child. "A.D.D." they'd diagnose it now. Between serving Latin mass and rocking in front of the hifi absorbing the family collection of Clancy Brother albums, I was immersed in mysterious language from the age most children take up reason. But being a bard is not the kind of vocation even a strange child aims for. There's no counseling, no pie charts. The profession is badly marketed, completely misunderstood. Shakespeare did a terrible disservice, or more likely it wasn't Shakespeare himself, but the bards—real ones—who came after. Shakespeare was no bard. He broke the cardinal rule: he became famous.

I'm not a bard like that with a capital letter and a prophet's beard and a college named after. I'm from a school created before nuns or whisky. We're teaching poets, beneath the high filí, who created the riddling rosc poetry—more obscure than Pound. The filí were ex-druids who loved sex too much to become monks, I think. Though word is the monks didn't do badly.

I've come forward now because I'm tired of all the whining. Everyone's complaining about the state of the art. There's no money in it. No one reads poetry. Universities have cloistered the great voices. Grim-faced essays take the patient's temperature, and there's even a book, *Can Poetry Matter?*, which pronounces the situation almost hopeless.

So I thought now might be the time to write down a few things I've heard, because when you know about bards, you'll know that the fellow stuttered when he framed his question. It's not *Can*, Mr. Gioia; it's *Is*. *Is* poetry matter. Is it good for you like broccoli or prose?

Bards take the matter out of poetry, take it off the page, away from the publishers and pundits, out of the libraries and cafe-conglomerate book-stores, and lodge it in memory, where many voices blend. Voiced, the poem is transfigured from a printed glyph to sensory language; ephemeral, but with a tensile strength derived from collective memory that births it. Critics may feel differently, but what matters to a poem is not how many times it is reprinted, but how deeply it penetrates into the heart.

The proliferation of bad poetry seems to frighten critics more than the prospect of steady labor. Maybe they're afraid that in such numbers not all the poems written can be stamped, and a few bad ones might get through and be mistaken for good ones, and then the ivy shivers. To grease the hand-wringing, I can only think of what one bard whose name I won't betray told us.

"I've got some good news and some bad news," he said. "The bad news is that 90% of the poetry you read is going to be dreck. The good news is that the 10% left over is enough to last three lifetimes."

What better way to filter out the dreck than to start learning the 10% by heart.

Learn by heart, I say. Not *memorize*. I am not a minstrel, not a professional performer. There's more to being a bard than memorizing. Memorizing is an act of will, but learning by heart is capricious. Minstrels memorize what they are paid to learn, so their performance is not a tribute to the poem. The heart doesn't enter in. They're lovely to hear, minstrels are, but they do no more than sing for their supper, which is why in the old days they were consigned to sit furthest from the fire with the mercenaries. Now, of course, they own castles.

There are stages in learning a poem by heart. The first is finding it. The best way to find a poem is to hear it in the voice of another bard. The experience can be so powerful that you learn the poem almost immediately; it brands itself into memory and you can hardly remember a time you didn't know it. Hearing James Wright recite Thomas MacDonagh's translation of Cathal Buidhe MacGilla Gunna's poem "An Bannan Bui," was like that for me. I can hardly resist it now: "The Yellow Bittern that never broke out in a drinking bout might as well have drunk..." But it's not the same. I haven't the heart for it on the page.

You might ask why I drop Wright's name when I shielded the other. That's part of the tradition: when identities mingle, as Wright's and MacDonagh's and Cathal Bui's do, names blends in a minor chord. You might feel this harmony when you hear a poem and find that in the one hearing it has become yours: as if you wrote it. Your identity and that of the poet blur, becoming irrelevant. I think of Robert Bly's translation of Kabir, "this is what love is like: suppose you had to cut your head off/ and give it to someone else,/ what difference would that make?"

Most people don't believe such a thing could happen to them. They think they'd have to do a St. Paul to learn a poem by heart after one hearing. But it's not a conversion experience. In bars and classrooms I've shown drunks and third graders how to do it. The poem I use most often to give people the experience of learning a poem in one hearing is a well-worn renaissance piece, so finely harmonized that it's anonymous. It's called "The Man of Double-Deed," and if you'd like to try your heart at learning, give this book to someone right now and have them read the poem aloud, once.

> There was a man of double deed,
> who sowed his garden full of seed.
> When the seed began to grow,
> twas like a garden full of snow.
> When the snow began to fall,
> like birds it was upon the wall.
> When the birds began to fly,
> twas like a shipwreck in the sky.
> When the sky began to crack,
> twas like a stick upon my back.
> When my back began to smart,
> twas like a penknife in my heart.
> And when my heart began to bleed,
> then I was dead and dead indeed.

Sometimes a poem doesn't take your breath away on a first hearing or you never hear the poem in the first place. Instead you find it on the page. There's another kind of pleasure, akin to mature love, in learning by heart a poem you've never heard spoken. You can compose the music of the poem in your own voice. Even if you don't have the excitement of a first hearing, you begin to feel after a while which poems need to be remembered. Whitman still soars, as does Williams and a surprising amount of Pound. Eliot, poor soul, can't flutter. But this is all bard room quarreling. You'll recognize the poems your memory yearns for.

Lift the poem off the page carefully, and don't strain to hold it aloft too long. I once visited the workroom of a bard in Wales; (Might as well admit it's Dylan Thomas—I can't shield a bard that big). Tourists filed past the shack on the banks of the Larne where Thomas worked, preserved just as it was before the White Horse. On the table was a tablet of handwritten poems—not his own, but Yeats, Herrick, Pope. I didn't have to be told what he was up to. He was lifting the poems off the pages of books and placing them down again in his own hand, leaving a diaphanous imprint on memory. Do it a few times till your thumb aches. Then you're ready for the next stage, which is to take the poem walking.

While learning a poem after one hearing feels like inspiration, learning a poem line by line while walking in its rhythms is as close as a bard gets to the miracle of composition reserved for the filí. Words tease, vanish, then reappear from nowhere. Paroled from the page, a poem might even reveal its source out in the open air. It's a strange experience. For one thing, if you're used to reading, your head's tilted differently. It takes some getting used to—seeing the sky, the trees, and fields—the very fabric of the poem—while immersed in a word-hoard. Don't trip.

Something happens when a line is being lifted for the last time from the sheet in your hand to its new and ancient home in memory. You feel the rhythm linking synapses that haven't before touched, redrawing memory's map, becoming yours. Afterwards, a tinge of that first walking might linger with the poem; years later you might glimpse a maple tree or a cloud sheering sunlight or a '69 Impala and you'll be set off, "Vowels plowed into other, open ground," or "I cannot think of anything today that I would rather do," or "Two evils, absent, either one apart." No earthly reason at all.

When you have a sheaf of poems by heart, that's it. You're a bard. There's no degree, no laurels. I hope you won't be as foolish as I've been about announcing it. I know you won't.

As much as I might like to christen a bardic school with all the trappings, it needs to be said that memory should never be held like a bludgeon over the page-bound. The oral tradition has its tyrannies. For one thing, it's hard not to learn by heart poems which seem to have been written with an audience in mind. The heart yearns for wholeness, and naturally chooses poems with a skin. Fragments of many states of mind—these are less memorable, but equally valuable. It is important not to rely only on the dramatic poems.

Poetry is not only, as somebody (I forget who) said, "memorable speech;" it is also the most forgettable speech. Unmoored by plot or character, its lack of reference can make for difficult remembering. This is especially true in this century when the mnemonic devices have become passé. Some poetry seems to be written expressly to prevent remembering. I defy his own mother to recite a hundred lines of Zukovsky, though *A* remains unparalleled, if unread. Sometimes I can open a book I've read and not remember a single poem, though it may be a fine book indeed.

The yearning toward the unsayable extends beyond what even the bardic memory can hold. They were always the filí's gifts and they still are. Perhaps being a bard is no longer a healthy full-time occupation. Maybe in this millennium we need to forget as well as remember. So it can be useful to try your heart in another way: see if perhaps you're not a filí. Experience failing at something grand is never wasted. Who knows? You might find your words sung one day by some Homer. Now there was a bard. Pity they put a name on him.

PROEM

from *Forged Correspondences*

First Born

The day the four McCann girls were shown Brooklyn
and told that beneath their feet were rivers and tunnels,
another fleet of trams, a whole underground city—
that was the day they realized they'd need me.

They could translate pence to nickels,
knew *mince* meant *raisin*, but one look
at the brickwork, the smoking girders—one look
at their small blue parents inching under the neon
storming the sky, and all but the baby sensed
they'd need an American—rich, educated,
tall if possible. But where to find one in the grease-
japped kitchens, in the kiosks, in the velvet sacristies?

On Sundays, Paddies in sloped work caps
leered at McCann's front stoop, greasers
sharked the boulevards, and Jews, garbed as mad priests,
muttered and cawed along the lanes of Prospect Park.
But the only way to get an American was to make one.

Mary was eldest so she tried first, but she barely had time
to squint at the house I'd rent one day
with turrets and stained glass windows opening into pine limbs
before the gardener she married,
whose tenor voice still trills in McCann memory,
died of rare cancer and their girl-child
started to swipe coins and grow black
crooked teeth not like me at all.

Then Betty the prim one entered
the plush mouth of the Savoy movie house
and when she exited daylight
swelled to rubies in her bleary sight, and that night
in her pillow she saw Africa: Bogart's bone deep
American gaze, and she, shimmying in the dream
out of her wool skirt, patting her curls.

All that summer she peered back
into the scum-white Coney Island surf
and then this Elizabeth, who skipped
over sidewalk cracks and steam-ironed her underwear—
she fainted, flailing the flexed waves
until a navvy flung his shoes in after,
and they lived like that, fainting and belting each other
while forty years skimmed by like a flat stone
and now she's babbling this fractured tale to me,
the sea meanwhile having shrunk to a damp shell,
but she's sure—my aunt—and still furious
that it was me thrashed out of her womb like a knife
(I nod, purr *sure*) and when she stiffens, spits out
that I fecked off the wrong way to some war,
came back someone else, I steal a glance
at my cousin's military snapshot taped
to the steel nursing home bed frame and swear
when it comes to this between myself
and me we'll shoot each other.

Then it was Kay who coaxed a wraith by jitterbugging
her flame fingernails; together they raptured
bars and K of C Halls then boogied home to make a me
Christ would mistake for his transfigured twin;
but I'd been craved so many times it was born
smudged—their whelp—padding the threadbare rug
in orthopedic shoes, getting religion,
soiling his musical necktie in the kitty litter.

And that left Pet the youngest who dreamt at first
of turrets and Bogart but finally
it was the dark she loved, mirrored
when she closed her eyes and pulled
a man down into it. That was the traveling then,
she could glide anywhere, the rivers and tunnels
farther than she'd ever seen or thought—no fear,

no need—and when she looked up I was gone—
for all the scams they brooded—
I'd slipped back, easy as a hanky through a ring,
though it must be
a sliver of me's lodged in the obscure god
who sprays graffiti and puffs black soot
on the crust of Brooklyn,
wildly fanning his worshippers back to life.

from *Weal*

Hindu

I don't know how they hand out incarnations,
but somebody got shafted with this one:
to be a handsome man without much brains,
bad heart, no money or position
in America in the depths of the cold war—
might as well be celery garnish or
a goldfish a kid's plopped in a vase
on the kitchen radiator. I guess
some feckless soul in Nirvana's holding tank
thumbing Brahmin mug shots must have finked
out the wrong guy, or flunked
a Rorschach test, or tumbled, drunk,
off some cosmic platform when the character
and fate of Edward Donlon roared
into him like a train and snuffed his bliss,
and set him on a life of accidents.
Or maybe that poor soul had a plan—
for, looking back on it, you can
trace his life's pattern as easily
as a glassed-in grid map of the BMT
after the graffiti's been scrubbed off.
And even if Donlon's life force got stuffed
into the hard luck carcass of a New York dick
with slattern wife, two whelps, and a thick
skull, he always dressed with style, strutted
his beat as if he knew where he was headed—
whether to the altar or the bar,
or down to the basement to wallop Eddie Jr.
In fact, right up to the Saturday he holstered
his service revolver, climbed the stairs
and locked the bedroom door
I doubt a single soul living on the block
thought anything was wrong—no shock
considering the cornice I grew up in—
Flushing, Queens—a post-war way station
of fenced-in postage stamp back yards,

row houses, unpithed hearts and T.V. dinners,
where the infirm of the hordes escaping Brooklyn
were culled on their stampede to the Island.
This was the true ground zero or ground nil
of scotch and casseroles—a lukewarm hell.
Our whole block hadn't enough prana
to incarnate an underfed amoeba.
There was Charlie Cast who BB'd passing cars;
Michael Stiefel, the owl-faced science nerd;
Leo Sarkissian of the pus-wet face,
LuAnne Piazza, goosed by Jamie Wallace,
tough guy, who explained it all to us
on the front stoop after Donlon died—
(it being both sex and suicide).
He sucked his middle finger, cocked his thumb
and fired, moaning, *a-bing-a-bang-and-a-boom*.
It was just one dusk in an eternity
of fireflies and casual cruelty.
Even the Police Force looked the other way
pretending accident, so wife Joan
could get the full-dress funeral and pension.
But because Donlon lived next door and died
a wall from my bedroom, and because I wed
his daughter, Maureen, at age ten,
in a giggling ceremony in the basement
where my kid brother played best man
in his communion suit, and because
I got dubbed Ed Jr.'s godfather and because
my father's spirochetic sperm embalmed
me safely unmade till after Vietnam
and because my lover's brother hadn't yet
hanged himself, and her tumor brooded
in secret, and because no one had ever been
or ever would be lost, Edward Donlon's
suicide shattered some trajectory—
like the arc of the Pensy Pinky

rubber ball you imagine already homered
out of sight as you step up to the sewer
with a broomstick. Foul it off, it's gone.
We called it a Hindu—a do-over—when the sun
blinked, the physical world wobbled free
an instant, and no one saw or could agree
on what they'd seen. The moment
Donlon opened fire into his open
mouth, when his incarnation exploded
into ether, or fumes, or light, or spumes of blood—
I think I was the only one to see.
I didn't see it then, exactly,
And I was far from the only ghoul
to replay that scene in prurient detail—
The coifed, spiffy corpse sprawled on the floor,
the wife and children petrified downstairs,
and later Joan, at the wake, soused,
muttering, "I didn't think he had the guts."
And Eddie Jr., damaged as his father,
saying to me, "I guess now you're my father."
No, what I saw developed slow
as a blond negative, slow
as a spectral x-ray of the splashy death,
the hum-drum life, and walleted beneath
Donlon's sharkskin suit, two secrets,
maybe the only valuables he kept,
and kept him separate from the sordid facts
he could not Hindu. The first was comic:
a rumor snaking through his drunken wake—
he wasn't a real cop: despite the gun
and badge and funeral and pension,
his fragile heart had failed the physical
and so he'd played cop as a transit mole—
a subway sleuth deployed underground to prowl
the detritus. And Donlon was not born
with a bad heart. That was the second

secret, second sight that cleaved him
from himself: a drunken night in the infinite
regression of lives before my birth that led
to his being next door, and that night led
to a car accident that killed his first
born daughter, Colleen, and nicked his heart
so that it wobbled, blinked. And this
is what I saw—Edward Donlon wandering
the flotsamed, numbed unconscious of Flushing,
Queens, dressed to kill, searching
for the snuffed-out essence my godson
was conceived in the upper world to clothe again.

Creedmoor

Between the overpass and institution wall
shadows snake across graffitied brick
and the tensile thrum of the Van Wyck
spells open their eyes. Thralled,

baboon-haired putzes thwock
handballs. Now floodlights click on
and I can name hallucinations:
Trush, Lebo, Gentile. One hundred

eighty proof. Three riffs on real.
Even a lifetime off no way I see
these three undulations coldcock every
particle of adolescent male

in Queens without a zing surging
up the spine, frazzling the ur-
layer of brain, and knifing toward
someplace where something

grotesque and unaccounted for
is about to coalesce. No diagnosis
can explain; no fist
protect. The place reason buffers,

The place you dream against.
We called it Creedmoor.
Not just asylum—a condition; a door
into borough zeitgeist

and a barb—"You're from Creedmoor, man."
We slouched against its wall. That's why
the floodlights beamed. That's why
tonight Trush flexes his skeleton

tattoo and Lebo's glare probes weakness
and Gentile, (whose name's as phony as

"Utopia" or "Fresh Meadows")
targets a knee to practice

kung fu on. Time—its pressure,
the detritus of things, the practiced lies—
you'd think they'd carbonize
old terrors, but now a cypher

squirms from the brick's maw,
face vacant as a future,
a half-demented creature—
Creedmoor, embodiment of flaw

gyrating like neon fog or a slinky
on the fritz. I've fingered three tough guys—
but now I watch the scene metastasize
searing the membrane between me

(if there's such a thing as me
in the fun-house-triple-mirror warp of rage)
and Creedmoor waving from beyond the edge
of light, screaming "mememememe"

in a nest of scabs and hair,
crazed syllables that some nights scan
as "antibodies," others as "napalm,"
sounds the world's made meaning for.

If he was only teased,
stripped, kicked and punched, spit on,
splashed with booze and stuffed into a can
that wouldn't light, it's because

the cops came in time—at least that night,
when Creedmoor drooled and babbled, failed to burn,
and I parsed myself among four primal forms:
inflicting pain, accepting it.

Myth

In the year of our lord when my lady classics prof
quieted class and flipped the light switch off,
and on the screen appeared celestial buttocks—
nymphs mounted by satyrs with huge cocks,
the scene all laced with whips and chalices,
she was maybe thirty—another species
from the tail I stalked: foxy virgins bent
on the MRS. It was sacred, she said, it meant
humans revealed as animal and spirit.
"Like a Phi Gam!" whooped one half-wit satirist.
So when she crashed the Kappa Sig keg blast
we bluffed it out. I was the classic douche,
so it was me got shoved forward to introduce
our Dionysian curriculum.
The sorry pup I was was almost numb
from slurping grain alcohol punch from barrels.
I was twenty, bent on being intellectual,
which meant disdaining parents, smoking a briar,
and really meant transforming into the satyr
Apollo flayed for challenging his music—
the god unstrung his heart, twisted his prick,
and disemboweled him with his sacred claws.
This was a week before my father paused
from typing my thesis to have a heart attack,
a year before a frat bro broke his neck,
another shot, and the rest scattered
to suburban bliss. This was before
spirits scotched pud and gnawed the liver—
the divine organ Greeks thought made us human;
before Marsyas, satyr, Apollo's victim,
switched pelts with me and left me taxidermed
to bark on hind legs behind a podium.
Maybe in the year of our lord of love
and my classics prof, I could have
morphed like Ariadne into tree;
if I'd translated Ovid right I'd be

a swan or mountain range or deathless spider,
instead of a trophy-mantle satyr.
Who knows? These days when I recall
my professor who said she was not beautiful
but was, who asked me to go home with her,
and I, not understanding, asked "What for?"
who spread a Greek myth picture book
before her naked body and said, "pick"—
I see my selves unrealized—
the river in that voice, the forest eyes.
The night she spirited me from the frat party
to be deflowered into mystery,
her arms engulfed, her thighs enraptured me,
she liquefacted me up into her womb,
but that ambrosia soon congealed to shame
when pals whistled, "You're one horny mother."
Then I graduated to my blood-typed father.
It was a failure to consubstantiate,
but something was conceived, and not weaned yet.
Now when I unhook paws from podium
and prowl bars, my plastered parts enflamed
to ravish nymphs, I feel her loneliness.
This was her mortal gift—to lace
fear and desire to flesh out myth.
I can't translate across that breadth.
Still, who knows? I might yet rage
and prance, hell-bent, through middle age.

Selkie

That water names as it disgorges us
is a catechism article of faith
and a cautionary tale from hit-man lure.
What separates the living from the found
is not the naming or the surfacing
but the momentary hovering over fate—
the element you can't breathe in or cling to.
Thus the breaststroke: a technique
to wave off phantoms, to clear the chuff
and afterglow of floaters that so cloy,
your goggles cake with rinds of chlorine film.
And so the rising, lapsing with each stroke
and so the laps in sonar waking dream
until the waving off becomes a sliding in,
and in a trance you find you've married water.
Because the stroke is outward, pushing away,
and because water is a body yielding,
you believe your bride is human and loves you.
She crawled from the surf and cut with a sharp shell
the seaweed cord. Yes, she was wed before
to some bull-seal, some king under the water,
but that was in another incarnation—
the only trace the salt stitched in her lips.
"Call him," you say. You want to fight
or bargain with this priapus of the deep,
blunt-headed, glistening with jism.
She mouths a skirl of bubbles and you fear
Your wife's husband stole away her breath.
His glandular pupil mulls the halogen lamp;
his belly slacks along the basin tiles.
Disgorged from mother's water by the shock
of his human father's drowning, he secreted
a proofed fur and dove in after. Together,
they brood the secret of being underwater.
It galls, entrances—the thought of going down
and being whole, pure sloth and ardor

in refracted light. You feel the undertow
as your lover jackknifes down to join her kin:
the mythed, the lost, that water won't betray,
and you—but for this breaststroke, this stretching
with a frog kick from the pelvis—you'd devolve,
limn fur, arms streamed to fins. You'd follow,
moving in water cleanly, tail clenched
so not to over-stimulate the sharks.
And nights drifting to sleep there would be this:
a selkie born the day a human drowned,
and mornings when your wife peels back her cowl
you'd glimpse waves obsessed with holding on—
all the missing would lour in your veins
down to the species lost in the first flood.
They're here, swimmer, furrowing eddies beneath
your tiring limbs, ready to anoint:
Last, and *Love to Death*, and *Precious Blood*.
Every breaststroke, with a kiss, they whisper,
"Marry water, stitch your lips with thirst."

Dawn

after viewing Sir Anthony's Gormley's Installation,
"Another Place" on Stravanger Beach, Norway

Fellow patrons of the first art nudie flicks,
first generation to witness explicit sex
in groups both ways in color since the Romans—
and this in the anno mirabilis '69,
women as well as men rapt, sucked in
by the plush neon bijou movie mouth
or pussy or ass—each word, each ticket punched
a gesture of political liberation—
thus Swedes, using only Copper Tone
and dialogue from Strindberg, could fashion
a cult classic—*I Am Curious (Yellow)*,
and *Heat*, a domestic release, could show
male and female genitalia unpruned
not just in Nirvana and Berkeley but behind
venetian blinds of row house suburbs
and in public on weekend nights with neighbors,
nodding to Fred and Holly, Biff and Estelle
queueing to enter visions of Blake's Hell
and some of us not old enough to drive.
No wonder we art-loving nudie buffs could brave
Mutually Assured Destruction, consciousness
strip pokered past the final guess—
bucking in velvet, our eyes exploding X's,
we watched creation french apocalypse.
And in the seventies the need to titrate
up the level of pheromones, and yet
at the same time maintain the veneer
of art—redeeming, transformative—not Lear
exactly, but a bit at odds with weather,
led Parisian director Just Jaeckin
to subtitle *Emmanuelle* "God is coming"
and she was, and his sepia Gothic S&M
Story of O climaxed with a scream
dissolving on the tortured woman's
canines, as if in this lacquered gleam

we glimpsed the eye of the mind's hurricane,
the radiance beneath Eve's fig,
source of Kali and sheela-na-gigs.
And some of us, floating from the theatre,
hands sticky with spunk and chocolate bars,
walked the earth for years clothed in
a trance lush and ineffable as the screen
images that strung our chromosomes
around the G of flesh and art, and now
I know that through the eighties when video
sex caught on and the nineties when theorists
lectured scrums of sophomores till they tsked,
a few kept walking, though their bodies bloated
or drank wind, though spiders clawed
their cheeks, though they left behind for dead
all women and any man who deviated
from erect posture or expression of awe—
such was their faith they would mature
perfect they kept on all the way here
to Stravanger Beach in Norway where they stand:
a hundred bronze sculptures sunk in sand,
green with salt wind, in sea foam,
their cocks twitching at the flush horizon.

Priest Hole

For Amir Or

After hours laying hands on the English
from his Hebrew in a twilit Scottish keep,
the poet reads my palm. A mass of runes—
that's all I ken of the weal I offer daily
to my mouth, but he has travelled to India
and beyond, and of dark arts, this he has chosen:
light beyond words. His own?
Branked for centuries, his poem's tongue
now quivers the far lip of consciousness
and in the timeless half-light of midsummer
I feel it coalescing, like new weather.
We are almost fully darkened with *Loch Dhu*—
black Scotch gone blind from aging in charred barrels.
Beyond? The poem's vanished. The last word
beckons to the darkness, "Speak."
The poet takes my hand. It opens
for the first time like a page. "Your future
cleaves," he augurs, "here," and he kneads a wen
forking from the pulse. "Now you choose one."
We've spent the evening sentencing
English and Hebrew to mad castling,
crabbing from opposite margins
toward a language just reborn, where One's
immense, omnipotent, and present tense
engulfs eternal twilight like *Loch Dhu*.
Each choice effaced the step below
until it seemed I stood on the lip
of a fell parapet, arms stretched.
Above, miasma of stars whispering
to the infinite. Below, fierce
ogham cuts; echo
of English iron striking stone.
I take back my hand. It steeps
in a smidgeon of unearthly light.
Here is a callus called *Mound of Venus*,
horned grain whorling to the first
stroke of eternity; here *Solomon's Ring*,
skinned escutcheon figuring loss and speech;

Here *Girdle of Saturn*, aura of fury,
crowning the fate that blossoms from a fist.
O God of gnostic grammar who parses time,
I did not know your power to glean flesh.
Now I will climb down, tonsure my pate
and trace Kabbalas between touch and pulse.
Only this I beg—let me keep
one venial future furled. Let one hand
dirk its pocket for a hole. Call it
the castle's Priest Hole, where hermits
mumble while hordes slaughter above
for the One Truth. O Laird, pray let
my five anchorites scrive unshriven walls.

Lunday

This is a last chance midnight A.P.B.
for my fugitive, one Robert Lunday,
last heard from four years ago in Japan
where he eloped with his ESL student
name of Yukiko, and infant, Dugan.
Last word I had was a letter saying he whored
part-time in a Kyoto K-Mart, a job procured
by his wife's tattooed Yakuza hitman father.
Last word, the scam to fence unknown
priceless paintings cut-rate had gone
under, and the stranded family was holed
up in a cold-water beach house and they'd sold
his father's watch to pay the bills. For me,
for anyone else I know, this would be
enough plot to distill a lifetime's stories,
but for Lunday it's just the latest and I hope
not the last scrape in a series of funky trips
that curlicue from Georgia, Soho,
Zaire, Oregon, Houston, Palo Alto—
(with a few side jaunts to parts unknown)
a wobbling arc of a friend exiled from home.
But really, there was never a home to leave.
His father, an Air Force hot-shot, died to save
his best friend on their second tour in Nam,
but some time before that the best friend
had married Lunday's mother, who then
cooked Thanksgiving dinners for both men
and a Vietnamese wife or perhaps it was
the second wife who cooked Vietnamese
and the second husband, Lunday's stepdad,
who spanked my shadow brother to manhood
and left his car in the short term lot and fled
in a piper cub with some vets or drug runners
never to return. Something like that. His sister
married a biker doing time on a murder
rap and Lunday heart-brailled all this

in a long, savage poem, "Major Lewis"
voicing the parabolas of loss.
Normally, I wouldn't borrow his thunder,
But I can't find him without an SS number
or his mother's first name or his sister's
married name or what prison she visits.
There are seventy Robert Lundays on the internet,
so far I've tracked down thirty-seven.
I fear he's dead. It would be just like him.
This is a man who left the Peace Corps
after two weeks because he was heart sore
for a woman he'd just jilted. Needless to say,
she jilted him right back for Hari Krishna
and was last heard from dancing jigs from Sarah
Lawrence to India and so Lunday Huck Finn'd,
shagged sheep on an Adventist farm, and landed
at sea in a commercial fishing trawler
puking tuna under Pacific stars.
That's when his step-father went AWOL and Lunday
was gill-hooked back across the country.
He tried everything to find him—Private Eyes,
Fortune Tellers, even the State Police—
maybe that's next—me hounding my old friend
across unearthly borders with sirens.
Although I'm elder, it was me who followed—
you can see that in our only photo—
the burrowing shoulders of him, the seriousness
of his allegiance, not to me, but to the space
he yearned toward, his visage fibrillating through
emulsion. And me, a weedy comma,
draped over, clinging like kudzu. Hunger
beams from me. I am Ugolino's tower
gnawing other's secrets, their starved words.
Maybe I followed Lunday because my blood
kid brother Brian had circumvented
primogeniture with his panache. He wed

his college sweetheart, entered corporate
heaven—he was sealed in luck—dipped to the heels,
ever since the Beehive—the posh preschool
our parents yellow-paged so Brian
could get a toddling start in the fast lane.
Meanwhile, Lunday and I adopted a scorched
earth policy regarding fathers—search
and destroy—then resurrect in verse—
starting with the two assigned to us—
then blowtorching the b.'27 gang—
Hall, Snodgrass, Kinnell, Wright, Dugan—
Dugan, yes, Alan Dugan, who the son's
named for. Once, Lunday brought home
John Logan, whom he'd found wandering
bookstores like Christopher Smart in slippers begging
copies of his out-of-print masterpieces.
"Here's one," says Lunday and produces
a first edition of *The Zigzag Walk*
from his knapsack. Signed. Robert, we've sucked
that marrow dry. Watched as fathers sank,
their torsos thrashing in Parnassian muck.
I'm bald now, still childless, paunching.
My brother and I did the American thing
dropping our parents in a suburban grave
beneath one of the humming techno-hives
where Brian pit-stopped on his speedy climb
(their corpses shift in my skull's slime
like bad teeth) and I have tenure
in a valley of molten fire.
All this is absolutely normal
and should have been almost visible
from *la plage* of Lake Kivu in the pre-dawn mist
where we smoked *chauvre* in banana husks
and guzzled from clay gourds of *lutuku*.
Mobutu called it Zaire then, Bukavu—
since exposed and razed on network T.V.

as yet another prime-time atrocity—
but then, for a few instants, it whirled
around and through us, bright, ineffable.
We saw pythons, masks, strange stars—
once, we might have glimpsed gorillas
on the mountains of the moon. But they seemed less
exotic than the fact of our own breath,
which only our words and futures could confirm.
Yes, we said, babbling on while dawn
made lucid the rippling lake and mountains
beyond—refract, don't let forms reify,
don't ogle and describe, don't stay
still, for fear of shrinking the world's vastness
to a fetish and titrating the synapses
to maps. But I did stay, till the heart's blister
cooled and now I don't care anymore—
to find my friend I'll make a fetish of him—
I'll write flat out, direct—I'll even rhyme
for the lit rags we sneered at for rejecting us.
Maybe some harried editor has news of you,
or some schlemiel dickering his pud
in the waiting room of the Dillard,
Georgia, impotency clinic
will read, engorge, recalling your antics.
To track you, I'll unravel my old yarns—
how I saw six falls where Mungo Park drowned,
how I tried to chisel Rwandan diamond smugglers
with Dime Savings Bank of Brooklyn rubber
to ferry me across Lake Tanganyika
and wound up dumped off in savannah
at the mango tree where Livingston met Stanley.
Lunday, I'll find a use for poetry.
I remember the morning you set out to swim
too far, and I remember the poem
where you almost drowned, were fished out
of the lake by smirking Lubas and vowed

to try again. I hope you've landed somewhere—
even if in a track development in Yonkers.
Even if you're living like a WASP
with a nub of cancer and stock market gossip,
some Chivas and an occasional fling
with the neighbor's missus. Your yearning
might have taken you too far, too deep
to hear. I don't ask much. Only I hope
you're alive, brother, gripping a piece
of the spinning earth we once thought we'd compass.

Siena

This morning, an American girl of five
living in England wakes for the first time
in the city she was named for. Her father
worked ten years for this one week
wandering Italian fields and vineyards,
playing at being home up to his knees
in sunflowers, his shades scanning the dream
landscape his parents cursed and left. Siena
fists her eyes; her mother pads barefoot
across the room and opens shutters wide
on morning in this medieval *campo*:
walls that gave a name to burnished clay,
bricks stained darker clay from blood
of men and horses that rage this afternoon
each year in ritual war called *palio*,
pounding as if to breach the earth
that made Siena's walls. Fear,
obscure as Etruscan graffiti
crabbing the gate's arch,
socketed each parapet with slits
and for a thousand springs Siena fixed
her eyes on crows pecking vineyards
and sunflowers, and beyond, on the clay walls
of Monteriggioni and Firenze,
as if each town were the brow of a red skull
pounding, each spring, until clouds
withered and men rushed out knee deep
in sunflowers, each skull dreaming itself
free from names. I hold Siena's hand;
this child who lives in England presses
close in the sunlight of Italian spring;
we cross the flagstone canyon of the campo
and she stares at spangled *cavalieri* preening
on ornamental horses, their crow-feathered lances
tapping the clay walls. She cries. What
gallops in Siena's skull? Will her skull

one afternoon one Spring be pressed
by pounding of a thousand names until
it chinks and fissures like a sun-scorched cloud?
I lean and whisper, "This is just the sky
and walls and towers telling a story," and she
cries and hugs my waist; the horses, teeth
to tail, glide round the *campo's* circle
like carousel wolves and lions, their gold
carapaced torsos fixed by lances
to the clouds. And my friends—
though they worked ten years in exile for one week
in the city that becomes each year the brow
of a red skull, though they named
their first child as if they meant to breach
a thousand springs and hear the original
silence in these walls—my friends stroll;
they tap stone eyes of wolves and lions
pouncing to life from the *Palazzo Publico*;
they turn to see Siena fist her eyes
under the stained glass of the *castellari*
where St. Catherine flayed her breasts to mingle blood
with Christ's. Is the world a siege
pounding their skulls? Would towers
crumble round their knees to hear
their story? It's a story
Siena's neighbor Dante might have leaned
to hear when names pounding his skull
breached the earth beneath the city
he was exiled from. What would he say,
treading a landscape rutted with iced
skulls and burning sunflowers, to these
two lovers who, to mingle flesh, fled walls
mysterious fear raises far away—
suburban parapets, billboards socketed
with pastel eyes—America—
where to lay siege or be besieged

inside the skull sometimes must seem
the only choices? I hold Siena's hand.
We watch the horses flay their riders' thighs
against the walls, each costumed horseman
racing this afternoon each spring
as if hooves could pound the dead
and living skulls into one dream: Siena's
vineyards and sunflowers blooming, withering,
reborn in one flashed spark. The story pounds
the flagstones but my skull won't blossom
into wound. I pass through cities
nameless, skimming earth, nowhere opening
my flesh to mix with flesh. This afternoon,
holding Siena's hand, I turn from the *palio*
toward arched passages of burnished clay
and if my whispering could breach the earth
I'd lead her down to name anew
each cornice, every flashing cell,
and laughing, watch them fade, so when
my skull withered to cloud and my hands clawed
like the hands of nightmare crows, Siena could
let go, rise shimmering like colored glass
and gazing inward whisper,
"My God, what have we left? What have we left
my child, but this, our only country?"

Proof

Across three continents in two envelopes
I am carrying, to remind myself,
proof that human creatures,
manifest in such numbers that God sneezes,
compose the simulacrum of one absence
incandescent beneath knowing so we stare
with horror and desire at ourselves.

This evidence consists of emanations
from past lives: six-hundred-forty-four
bundled articles of V—MAIL
exchanged between a G.I. and his bride
from nineteen-forty-two to forty-five,
each dispatch stamped with censor's seal,
and opening with diminutive salutation:
"Dear Stardust," or "Dear Moonbeam;" sometimes "Dearest."

I bring these letters to their furthest points
of origin and destination: Bohemia,
the very pencil mark, later erased,
where The Big Three planned to dissect Europe,
before posing, seated for Roosevelt's sake,
like a row of schoolboys—Stalin roguish,
Churchill flashing his signature V for Victory,
a voodoo of the index and fuck-you finger
designed to hasten what it signified.

I lay them in two shallow holes I've dug
under a shade tree at Vitezné Námisti,
a crossroads in a village of stucco
whose name means Victory Place,
but which, to me, echoes Vietnam,
dissolved into the temporal
as Lidice transliterates to My Lai:
with the twist (like the flick of the wrist
morphing Churchill's "Victory"

into bohemian "Peace") that the humans
whose destiny I share are killers.

This Place of Victory in Bohemia I found
not by addresses, masked by Army code,
nor history—writing and erasing names
in a trance of organized forgetting.
I found it tracing glyphs and curlicues
of turquoise and black India ink
first pored over and passed between two forms
who have dissolved into this present act.
I am their proof: the son these letters caused,
in a future just beyond my earliest past.

Here, in letter three-hundred-seventeen
Moonbeam asks her Stardust to list towns,
villages and hamlets he had passed through.
It was October 23, a Tuesday.
Sinatra's voodoo bathed the railroad flat.
Moonbeam's gaze drifted out the window
where the wind revealed Stardust in shivering leaves
and she realized she'd finally passed the point
where she could stare at a vacant Brooklyn street
without the features of her lover
taking form. Absence voodood
as leaves, as radio waves, longing so deep
its anonymous face is manifest only now
when the moon, for example, no longer signifies
"spontaneous overflow of emotion"
and stars don't stand for "stake in the eternal."

It's only when the idiom wobbles
and the meter stretches at the seams as in
"across three continents I am carrying"
that human creatures stir and almost wake
to the absence incandescent underneath,

the way the ocean suddenly disappears
from the limbic mode of the farmer as he kills
the Russian tractor's motor
that gurgled all morning through wheat fields
around Place of Victory, and he's lost—
overcome with a surge of sourceless longing,
perched dizzy but alert in wheat so high,
the tires barely top the tawny waves.

That's proof. That's one reason I sow
fetishes in separate holes—
to let them try, impossibly, to bleed
into the shade tree's roots, which I declare
for purposes of my voodoo, earth's neurons,
forever so achingly absent,
this Place of Victory shimmers, disappears.

The second reason I pock the crux of Europe
with a penknife and two envelopes is the third
continent these letters have furrowed.
It is called memory. It is a distant
palisade stippled with barbed wire.
And on this continent the absences
whose carbon-fragile longing's buried here
squat, long past horror or desire—
a pair of torpid gods facing the sea.

And human creatures rage over this proof:
that memory resisted or erased
bleeds, bathing neurons with longing
to reconceive whatever we bury
in pliable shapes—wind and leaves and words.

This may explain the gleam in Stalin's smile
as he peers into a future his pencil's pushed
until everything but absence is erased:

Victory, Bohemia, the entire
continent of memory distilled
to names scrawled and buried so deep
in separate holes longing dissolves
into the tractor gliding like a moon,
the revolution climbing to the stars,
and not a single body to obscure
how close we absent are. How present
and alive. He leans toward us. He almost sees
the source of everything that won't be born.

Monument

For Isabelle Meglinky

Now she is dead, I speak to my mother in French.
Her strokes and the strokes she nursed my father through
revealed the future: I'll die by nonsense,
my English thickening to the tongue of a shoe,

so I practice now, rerouting synapses
and teaching her dead synapses to spark,
although she spoke no French, and mine consists
of a few rote phrases that M. Laroque

(who, in our myth, was once a general
in the Haitian army) drilled into us
in high school, when it seemed impossible
to die, or care, or salve our loneliness

in any language. When she lived,
I spoke to her in scrawls, mailed from beyond
the sill of her world and so encoded
with desire they hummed mantras

as they yellowed on her freezer.
Now I'm no mystic and my grammar falters,
but here in the autumn foothills of north Georgia
I speak to the living image of my mother.

She comes to me as a Parisian sculptor,
but shaped so like my mother—
her eyes, complexion, cheekbones, hair, and gesture,
I would believe she were the answer

to some prayer if I prayed or believed
any God would bother with a two-card-monty
miracle. I know we are all carved
from the same flesh. And we all die

once, alone. My mother takes my hand
to show her art—her sculpture in the hills—

seven pillars raised from stones strewn
on the winding path from her cabin to the sill

of the world, where she has braced a bridge
of dead limbs veering into space. How explain
such labor? Such coincidence?
Who will see the seven guardians

balanced, impossibly, like minotaur spines,
or helixes of the planet's DNA,
or tombs, fragile dolmens—
holes inversed from darkness to convey

what? My mother will not speak. The sculptor
bends to scrawl in clay, *le temps fini
disparu dans l'infini du temps.*
The stones tense at my touch; the bridge sways.

Lagos

My younger brother, orphaned, phones
past midnight from the West to warn
that Lagos is fatal to travelers.

These months I haven't stopped moving
and even in sleep my eyes
need a constant downward
and eastward pull.
                        He reads the warning sign
in three languages at L.A.X., and says
I must not go.
                        I listen
but can't follow anything that gives up
short of the far margin.
                        When the doctors
finally gave up, my mother was elevated
to the top floor and I was let
sleep with her in an empty wing.

What dream makes me fear rising?

I need midnight to be spirited
over silences like sidewalk cracks
until sounds slip destination
and walking is just falling
in step.
            I could easily have gone
with my first brother: this my mother
murmurs in my dreams
in morphine tongue.

But I thought I was eldest.
                        These months,
booze and book gloss honeycomb
the inside of the skull.

                    Downward
and eastward, Lagos
is a hive of unknown millions guidebooks
compare unfavorably to Cocytus.
                              Sleeping
in the hospital with my mother
was closer than I've ever been
to anyone though I seldom touched her.

She didn't always know
which one I was—sometimes she thought
I wanted blood so she would turn
her head into the pillow and hold
out her left arm.
                    I was a blue
baby, transfused eight times
in my first two weeks of life.
My mother called me
distant and often joked
I was a changeling.
                    At night
in the empty wing I sang
her songs and sometimes words
channeled through me from the honeycomb
of rooms below my feet.
                    God knows.
Is that good? I'll be right back.

My brother and I crashed into each other
from opposite shores each cigarette break.

It was me stranded in California then
and I phoned in almost every breath.

My voyage is conducted by the eyes,
but memory seeps, silting up

the delta of the optic nerve. Then
words give up.
                    The doctors
gave up after the third intubation.
Intubation is a word but when remembered
it is my mother's face incarnate,
it means shut off from air and speech.

A priest translated—sometimes my mother
thought I was this priest
and turned toward me like a sunflower
toward light.
                    In Lagos
traffic and gas fumes murder sleep.
I have touched down
in a city of three languages,
all slurred.
                    If only to recall
my mother's face turning toward light
I'll translate now: trauma
means suffering if it's someone else's,
even if you once nestled in her wing.

In Lagos my eyes move downward
and eastward against dreams.
                              Movement
is a mantra.
            Dopamine is a number
telling how tight the human network's
stretched.
              If you've seen Lagos
traffic you know what it means
when tubes are forced down a living

throat.
        Memory seizes.

                    Sleeping
with my mother means
her death.
                If
my father's low sperm count
hadn't kept me formless until after
World War II experiments with RH factors,
I'd have choked on my own blood.
                                        Death
can be hilarious.
                        The last thing
she said was, *Don't cry you're getting me
all wet.* And before that—
she whispers it each night into
my sleep—Where is
my first born?
                        She liked morphine
and when she wasn't being made
to breath by machine, she said
reproachfully, *This
is what drugs should be for.*
                                Can secrets
conjoin us without flesh?

The doctors said don't worry
how horrible it looks, she probably
won't remember.
                        When I
remember, the earth skids
and veers, the mind
seizes and suddenly I'm jumbled back
in intense sun under the Ujiji
mango tree where Dr. Livingstone
  encountered Henry Morton Stanley.
                                Coincidence
sparks a fleeting sexual joy.

                              I travel
ear to the vanishing,
the way my brother
records his kids shilling ditties
on his answering machine.
                         Sometimes
in rage we call each other
Father in a kind of mythopoetic
Who's On First.
                    I didn't sleep with my mother
but lay awake listening to her breath
like fast spondees; she was down
to that—just breathing—and I knew
each breath was made by the fiction
of one thing following another
we call memory.
                      From Lagos, I follow
the river to the Emir's Palace near the ford
where Mungo Park drowned.
                               Can tides
quell fear?
               I returned
to the top floor and the doctor
was already there—in hospitals
they're kings—it's unbelievable
they can walk under
the weight of so much awe.

He was diffident; he'd risen
to Marin General from the Bronx
and he saw this Brooklyn mother and her son
and felt, maybe, just faintly,
that but for luck he might have been born
me.
      Me, that is, the one,
                      by miracle,

blue blooded, christened
maybe in past lives as
Mungo or Henry Morton—
                  that's the trick—to step
into that one
of a billion incarnations that won't
madden.
        The doctor said
he liked poetry
            and for that
incarnated instant I felt human
as if my mother's body were still
free, her gaze
deepening as the jacarandas brightened
in the window—
            there's nothing like Marin—
the hospital cafeteria is a bistro—

and I would have done anything,
anything in the world to please
him, to coax his words
into my mother's living face.
            The Emir's
Palace has no running water, but his word
knits ninety villages together.
            Dreams
ascend to congest the pineal gland.
            Lagos
is a labyrinth—it swallowed
eleven billion dollars in windfall profits
from the Gulf War and it's still
famished.
        Even the desert's
breath, the harmattan,
dies in its maw.
        I returned

to the top floor from a quick smoke
and the elevator hissed open as usual.

Choosing that my mother die
instead of breathe
by machine is a memory, but dreams spasm
silent as heat lightning—I can wind up
anywhere unless my eyes
keep moving.
            I travel to describe
an arc: an ark rocked by cloud-
exploding storm.
                My father died
three weeks before my mother
visited California, and on days
the morphine thinned and she remembered
that he went without a word or a glance back,
she said she felt like a stranded Baucis.
                            One night
the capital was spirited from Lagos
to the beautiful planned city of Abuja.

I found my mother naked
in intensive care, her face
wedged between gurney
and night table, her right arm spasming
like a crippled moth.

It was the first time
I ever lay down
with her. It was the first
time nothing mattered, just
live.
        Heat rises
from Lagos dirt streets past midnight.
Even at night my skin itches and burns.

In the hospital my mother talked with ghosts
using her right hand as a phone.
I learned by eavesdropping
on morphine I am not
her first.
                    Livingstone missed
the true source of the Nile, but followers
carried his bier reverently to the sea.

Let the sea churn.

When the Emir enters, his peacock
miraculously unfurls, each quill
distinct, the great fan sweeping
the Aegean eyes in a design of moons.

My mother always wanted to be a wren.
She sang herself a cautionary lullaby
about a mother who murdered her baby
and was hanged.
                    I sing to remember
one thing following another, but I can't
thread words.
                    My mother never abandoned
her first ghost.
                    He lived
with the wrong blood only
a week, and so I took
his name.
                    Lying
with her in intensive care and later
with her body breathing
from memory on the top
floor, I only
wanted to unsleeve my skin.

The string
they call the lifeline is frayed blue.
Maybe I'll unfurl.
                         No one
knows exactly what happened.

My mother thought she was going to see
her mother, she said her mother
loved her the way she loved me, but by then
I wasn't sure exactly who she talked to.
Seven villages claim the spot
where Mungo Park died.
                         When my elder
brother died, he left
a trace of longing deepening
in my eyes.
             I found him
forty years too late as in
some treacly Dickens plotline
winged with harps.
                    From Lagos,
America seems heaven. For funerals,
they slaughter seven cows, but their
cows look like starved kine of Exodus.

Undertakers have an underground
air network—they drain
the blood, apotheosize clients
20,000 feet, then sink six—like
counterclockwise Christs.
                          Maybe I'll go.
Maybe a brother needs me. I don't know
where I'd be with my own blood.

There are days I prefer the swimming pools,
the palms, the sweet order of Abuja.

One morning I rose to the empty wing
and she was gone
and though she'd wandered
the morphine labyrinth
for weeks, I don't know
what broke free, if anything
ascended westward, or if
she looked back, but if
she did, if this was
Euridice,
          there was nobody there to wave goodbye to.

from *By Heart*

Ginsberg in Ballydehob

There is a pub in Ballydehob, West Cork, called Leviss. It's a small shoebox of a place with a dry goods shelf, a deal table and three raw chairs, a hirsute recliner, and four stools knuckled up to the bar. Leviss is run by two spinster sisters, Nell and Julia—two beautiful old ladies straight out of "The Dead." They've owned the pub as long any hobbit remembers.

Nell and Julia conduct business, if you call it that, the old way—shuffling in from the parlor to pull your pint, with a "Now my good man;" "Yes my girleen." But for some reason the "Celtic Tiger" seems mesmerized by this old shebeen. If you're Irish, if you've been to Ireland, if you're anyone, you've been to Leviss. Mary Robinson sat in that recliner; Van Morrison guzzled on that stool. The photo of Nell and Julia in Pittsburgh Steelers T-shirts was taken by Dan Rooney, the Steelers' owner, and last night the gent sitting next to me introduced himself as John, the Chancellor of the University of Alabama. I'm told there's even a sign in an Irish ex-pat bar on the Upper East Side pointing east: "Leviss 3000 miles."

Of course, if you're Irish, if you've been to Ireland, if you're anyone, you know this. You know (though you never heard it from Nell or Julia) Kevin Costner's had a pint here and John Hurt drops in and John Minihan drinks here (have you seen Minihan's photos of Beckett?), and John Montague regularly waters his Jamesons at Leviss.

I'd like to think that Allen Ginsberg once sat crosslegged on the sawdust floor of Leviss. It's an old West Cork name, (pronounced LEE-viss) but once a tourist is said to have asked Julia, "Leviss? That's Jewish, isn't it. Are you Jewish?" Without a blink, Julia replied, "Yes we are." I'd like to think Ginsberg heard that story. He loved Ireland—Ginsberg did—I'm told. Once, he flew to Dublin to read without fee because the Director of Poetry Ireland, Theo Dorgan, offered him an Irish tweed suit. Theo says Ginsberg was buried in that suit.

The reason I want Allen Ginsberg to have been to Leviss is that I think he may be the last American poet who was anyone. I don't just mean that his name is one of the few poet's names since Whitman known to the general public; I don't mean only that he was a cultural as well as a literary figure. I mean that with Allen Ginsberg died the idea of American poetry as a story that could be kibitzed in bars like Leviss. Of course, it was Ginsberg and the Beats who challenged the story of American poetry, but that's part of the plot too: in challenging, they left it a better tale than before.

It was all explained to me at Leviss one night after closing time, blinds drawn, by a famous Irish poet. If you're anyone, you won't need to be told who.

"You had your New York poets—Ashberry and Merrill and O'Hara and that crowd," he declared, "over here;" and he slid the dregs of a Murphy's pint due east.

"And Hughes in Harlem and Williams just beyond." He thumbed two creamy circles on the bar. "And Bishop up north in the woods," he said, scaling a tri-cornered coaster against the base of the Smithwick's tap, "and Lowell too—grappling his spectral Hitler up in Cambridge.

"Then you had the Chicago gangs," he tapped a matchbox by the tureen of water, "Lee and Brooks and the other ones—Kunitz and Resnikof—the Objectivists. And above," he pointed toward the bar's laurelled mirror, "there was that mad Protestant farmer Robert Bly, and the Ohio footballer James Wright with their Deep Image.

"In the middle, the Iowa bowsers," he downed a wee jag and pucked the tumbler down, "top-guns flown in from everywhere by Henry Pussycat, who plotted for decades to murther Cal.

"Down here," he snapped a pound coin on the bar, "the Southern gentry—Penn Warren, Tate and Ransom.

"And out there," he continued, taking a gulp of Leviss's rough red vintage with his left hand and rocking the western goblet on its base, "The rebels and mumbo-jumbo mystics, Reed and Duncan, Rexroth, Snyder and Ginsberg—with one ear cocked to Nirvana and the other to Gotham."

Finally, with the topography of America completely consumed, he lurched hard left and tamped his fag in a scalloped ashtray, hard as a period.

"And there was Merwin in Hawaii—an extinct volcano."

This was the America this famous Irish poet had been reading for forty years like a palimpsest. It's the America I was taught to read also by some of the very poets nestled in the pints, ashtrays, tumblers and wineglasses littering Leviss bar. It's a story that enriches this famous Irish poet's sense of his part in a great drama. Reading it once filled me with desire to enter its alluring web. It's a story that seems to have unraveled. He asks me, finger wagging, "Who are your contemporaries?"

If an Irish poet were asked this question it would make for a night's great craic. "There's Yeats up in his eyrie and Kavanagh like Antaeus slagging him to earth and Clarke the failed priest and Devlin who almost passed for Turkish, and then the phalanx of Papists: Kinsella, Murphy, and Montague. Finally the tinder explodes and the Northern generation springs up from dragons' teeth:

Longley, Mahon, and famous Seamus (like a rock star or pope, known by first name only). You've got Carson and Muldoon hooking fangs, and Simmons, grandson of the Lord Mayor of Londonderry, reincarnated in Gaeltacht Donegal. Before you could turn your head Eavan Boland swats the whole male quiff off the story, flanked by Ni Chullinean, McGuikian and Ni Dhomhnaill—who reminds us that Irish is the only European language in which woman have always had a public voice. Then there's Cathal O'Searcaigh, who bills himself 'the Gay in Gaelic,' and the new generation of jackeens—Meehan and Boran, and the Cork boyos, Theo and McCarthy and Gerry Murphy the swimmer and Delanty over in the States with Grennan and Liddy."

If you're Irish, if you've been to Ireland, if you're anyone, you know all these characters, and you're bristling to elbow in some of the names I've missed.

Maybe there are still American poets who talk this way. Maybe, in this outpost beyond the beyonds nestled under Mount Gabriel, I'm so far from the new sources of American poetry I might as well be in Brigadoon. Maybe I just don't get it, and you're reading this with the polite boredom you feel for rustic relatives. "The barbarians are at the gates again, dear—this time I think they're Irish."

But I wonder, if you are my contemporary, if you read *AWP* and *Poets & Writers*, which blip their lighthouse signal promising "there is a story; there are prizes, fellowships, and spangles galore—look at the pictures, all is well," how would you answer the famous wagging finger? Who are your contemporaries?

It's easy to despair of making sense of the burgeoning poetry of this generation, of the three thousand books of poetry published every year, of the colonies and programs, the journals and special-interest anthologies, the work-shops and conferences, each advertised with its bespangled visiting faculty—prize adorned, internationally unknown. It's easy to feel that the story has been usurped by "Po-biz," a cynical bestowing of destinies on well-placed cronies. It's easy to feel that coffee-houses have been replaced by computer-generated class-lists. Looking at the wreckage of American poetry in the flotsam of Leviss bar, it would be easy to feel that American poetry is debased.

Perhaps the story finally became too good, had "too many notes," and could no longer bear the weight of its own complexities. Or perhaps I'm merely being naive: as Ginsberg's "Howl" took years to sink into American consciousness, perhaps there are readings going on right now which will seem, from the perspective of the early twenty-first century, to have been present in our minds long before most of us actually heard them. But then why is it that Irish poets seem to know the score? Why is it that when I talk to American poets we hardly even expect to share contemporaries?

If the story of American poetry has ended, there's much to mourn. Any story which entwines poetries of different times, places, and sensibilities encourages writers to learn from one another. A.B. Yehoshua has said that if someone came to Israel and asked about writers, the same five or six people would be mentioned; but visiting Chicago he was assured of the importance of hundreds of writers. And the same name was seldom mentioned twice. Of course the result was that he learned from no one.

Donald Hall argues that contemporaries stretch ambition. The story raises the standard since every new achievement is sifted through tradition. "In my generation," Hall writes, "we wanted to unseat Homer. Now poets only want to get published in *The New Yorker*." It's worse than that now, Mr.Hall—most poets swim far below that waterline.

While tradition may torque ambition, Leviss—or the Newyorican or City Lights or Naropa or Bread Loaf—can be very small places. They can produce the kind of inbreeding that desiccated European monarchies. Reading poetry the way it's taught in university courses, with anthologies and influences and movements—all the light shining on a few blessed constellations of writers—can be a cramping affair. The belief that poetic consciousness is invested in a few people apotheosized early in life by the likes of—I won't name them, but if you're anyone you know who the king&queen-makers are—is a life-draining belief. I'm not just talking about "multi-culturalism;" I'm not trying to unseat one story by saying there are many. I'm saying that investing poetry in certain consciousnesses, however many or diverse, keeps poetry exotic and apart.

Having a story to tell both enlarges and contracts the world. By connecting us with poets from all over the world, our minds are expanded. By insisting that poetry resides in those figures, the world is shrunk to the size of a map. The story stretches us to read what we would not have understood, but it also keeps most readers alienated from our own original readings. It helps us honor those who have lived rich lives in poetry, but it can inhibit an instinct that ought to be nourished: an instinct to read originally that was very much alive in the poets named here, poets who insisted that their reading as well as their writing be untrammeled.

Don't be fooled: original readings are rare. Few people read, as Yeats says poets must write, possessing "nothing but their own blind stupefied hearts." Reading originally is a gift almost as rare as writing originally. As students we begin by reading in the context of the story, and there's no doubt this is valuable. Who today would encounter Eliot or Pound or Zukovsky or even perhaps Ginsberg outside of the American story? But reading these seminal poets doesn't affirm one's identity unless the reader develops an ability to read with fresh eyes, open to the possibility that the next poem encountered might sustain imaginative life as well as *The Divine Comedy*. I'm not saying that there is any poetry as *good* as *The Divine Comedy*. But unless you can approach poetry with such a possibility in mind, you may be condemned never to feel the difference.

Am I suggesting a revolution? If I am, it's not to replace one set of icons for another, not to insist we install *these* poets in the canon and expel *those*. Maybe the best poems are those we have read originally.

So, my contemporaries, you ask? There was the woman in San Jose who wrote heart-wrenching lyrics, and my colleague at the University of Ibadan who opened his readings with Yoruba folk-songs, and the young poet I met in Maine ten years ago and have never forgotten, and the performance poet who electrified Binghamton, and my Ohio friends—the one who's written the definitive poem on appliances and the one who's written songs James Taylor couldn't lay a finger on. There's the poet who stands before an audience and dares us to "Give me a subject" for an extemporaneous sonnet. But you've never heard of any of us. Nor do you need to, since you must have your own canon.

What will drive our ambition? What will guide our judgment? How will we avoid simply becoming self-congratulatory without achievement, handing out plaudits to smaller and blinder cliques? For one thing, I don't think we'll stop reading Dante or Ginsberg. And I hope we're not foolish enough to believe that the poets in our town or borough or neighborhood or website are the unrecognized descendants of the Beats or Black Mountain or Objectivists or Dada. If we are wise and humble, we will acknowledge that it is finished. But we will recognize that in its ending, new possibilities blossom: perhaps we can read and write without allegiance to any movement, or better, with infinite allegiances. Our ambition will be different, but perhaps as great as that of our poetic ancestors: to live, for now, without the comfort of a story, to read each poem as if this one—against all odds—could be a catalyst to change our lives, though of course knowing that we will almost always be disappointed.

"The rest I pass, one sentence I unsay."

Finally, I too long for the story. Inflecting our own voices into tunes others will hum and humming tunes made long ago are deeply felt needs, and I feel them as I answer the wagging finger of the famous Irish poet.

So I tell him that the best poet of my generation, the one whose work I've read with the most joy and attention, the one who has changed my life, is Robert Lunday. We met in Zaire, mapped out our ambitions together, equipped ourselves to storm Parnassus as we crisscrossed paths from New York, Cork, Provincetown, Houston, Ohio, Oregon, and Berkeley, and I've lost touch with him in Japan.

Robert, I've written this for you because there are so many stories in American poetry, ours is garbled, and we can't even hear each other. If you read this, old friend, write to me, c/o Leviss, Ballydehob.

from *Fathom*

J'accuse

Here's the dilemma: The adolescent boy
rocking on the toilet seat, arms clenched
around his concave chest to numb his pulse
and focus on his immediate need to choose
between medicine cabinet mirror or water glass—
which to smash and how to gouge each wrist—
this boy, although he hums, although a wave,
blood-red, wells up behind squinched eyes,
can never meet the man who wants to save him,
though the man exists, speaks now, in riven voice,
haunting his tortured self from long ago.
The dilemma? How to blossom. Entwine
in self-renewing present, let the man
calm the boy's wrists, purr 'accord'
into the ear of the continuum.
Moments at a time perhaps, they join.
Then the glass shatters, blood spurts.
And who has broken the mirror or the cup?
The boy, despairing? The man arriving
thirty years too late? No. I accuse
the forward rush and press of language,
applied like a shard of glass to the boy's wrist.
I accuse myself for rhyming the tuneless hum.
I accuse you, who thought to remain hidden,
Reader, consisting only of eyes and nerves,
and a fan of fingers probing a bound spine.
You, Listener, I accuse;
though you are restless, caught perhaps
in bonds of collegiality or love
or trapped in auditorium folding chair.
You breathe with me; you yield to evanesce
into the scene, calmed by this voice—
this promise the boy lives—veiling
and sanctifying gore. Now you are named,
perched on the crest of porcelain
between worlds. Speak, my Reader;

you are no longer dark. Lift
a glinting fragment off the tile,
pinch between forefinger and thumb,
slice vertically along the bluish line
up toward the heart, which
I accuse—whose name
Blossoms in Blood, conferring
on every incarnation implacable need
to wrap numb arms around torso,
and yet to be released into unknowing.
The dilemma: within is contained All,
but what's needed to say All—
the palate, teeth, the eel-like tongue,
produces without meaning the word Other.
I accuse and stand accused of harboring
such sense as vouchsafes boy and man
forever separate. I accuse
the stream of time and self-fulfilling plot
of abandoning this boy who rocks uncradled
endlessly on the brink of blossoming,
the hum rising in pitch as he curls forward,
gurgling down the scale as he lurches back
to Original Unbeing, Primal Wound,
All-Encompassing Wholly Ceaseless Pain.

Wound

What if what the women told Freud was true—
the claws, the monstrous pricks, belonged to
living men? In the dead of night
a doorknob turns, undistilled
by nightmare. Afterwards, he lays
them out, the father of analysis,
penning into myth a torn nightgown,
transubstantial as a Sabine urn.

On a far shore, they stand,
"Father," they call. "Doctor
after anesthesia." "Satyr."
"Mask at knifepoint." "Husband."
I vow. I take my lover's hand.
She gazes back at me and says,
"I am incapable of feeling joy."

Is there a place where I am
not a man or woman?
Men cut to bleed,
longing to resolve to liquid.
Even God craves wounds.
Once, He spurted blood—
then struck. His son's
blued eyelids squinch in pain.

Dreaming, my mother slips into my bed.
She is more naked, being dead.
She is immune to touch. She cannot be.
"Will you still bear me,
bodiless," I ask, "when I cross over?"
I dream the day I stripped in our backyard
and dove head first in snow. I lust
still, and still the earth resists.

Mortal

Unseeable, unsayable, being dead.
But shadow-blooming iris, lip blooded—
I see and say. A child, I rocked
and hummed to dilate clocks.
Unplumbed, my tongue; but palpable
the pulse of subterranean ventricles
from Queens to Tokyo—turnstiles
ticking by the billions as deep as
Cocytus, where all suns clot.
What's mute, can names dilate?
The salt unseeable, where does it steep?
A key twitches my shadow, trickles blood.
An iris suddenly clots, the blooded word.
Unsayable, all future days unseeable
as unbloomed suns, even tomorrow furled.
My bones steep. Will we wake in time?
Does fear of not returning unfurl rhyme?
Unseeable, seeable, rain unsalting seas,
and steeping in my saline blood a key
to Queens or Cocytus. Sayable,
mute death, the day all ventricles
dilate. A child, I could pretend
I saw echoes. Time and darkness bend.

Gilt

Winter nights, dismissed from Fordham Prep,
I'd find him on the bus—Mr. McMann.
As the door hissed open and I stepped
into the vestibule and rendered a token

I'd feel his cloudy gaze. And even if
I snaked around the strap-hangers unseen
and sank between somnambulists
to conjure Mt. St. Ursulan prom queens,

by Utopia a force would push me up to
sit with the old man, my neighbor's father,
and lean and nod, attending to his gabble
until our bell got pulled. Then down the stairs,

and into the cold dark. Words can't express
the slowness of his gait. Out of time
it creeps over me now, as I cross
into the suburbs of old age. I make no bones.

What fixed my numb fingers to McMann
encompassed me: Ancestral Bulls
mandating the 6:00 AM alarm,
and the daily interborough busses

and the cramping desks where I cracked
Aquinas, and the waxy sandwiches,
and the jock-infested lockers, and the trek
across the desecrated corpus of the Bronx

back to Queens, where the row house door
snapped shut. *Caritas*, purred the Jesuits,
or *Agape* in advanced Greek seminar:
blossoming through others into Christ.

But all I felt was cold. Ruptured
sidewalks uncoupled our limp. We shouldered

into the wind to ford boulevards
and tottered under blind windows toward

a destination no doctrine can name.
I see us now, steering arm in arm
through the years to reach that occult haven—
gilt in traffic light as if blood-smeared.

Angel

An afternoon in autumn in mid-life.
You wander the empty house in thinning light.
Surf channels, water plants, sift
through unpaid bills until the habit

of being enveloped in skin
enthralls and you land face up
on the love seat, staring at the ceiling.
Hands drift to waist; unzip.

If, at the instant the skull
throbs lightning, the air,
weightless, reveals an Angel—
no, yes—there in a corner—

would you call it that? Why not sleight
of dusk? Or shame smearing eyeglasses?
Or tissue of a ghost teased out
of the wadded batting of the past?

And afterward in the auto-coital haze,
what if it stayed?—cloying like the close
November weather creeping in, days
that seep down crevices

like tears, which he licks, this voyeur
of the spasm whose filmy wings unfurl
around zero, then pince in to stir
the spent, shriveled pod tipped with pearl.

How he loves the way nothing obscures his view.
His gaze elides over the contours
of the aura, boring through shadow,
peeling away lineaments from the figure

lust conceived to clothe the chimeral womb
where eternity congeals—lusterless,

void. It's for this he's come—
to see creation shammed, the cosmos

thumbnailed. Unhinged seraph,
harbinger of null. The twilight chill
is his warped halo spindling for proof
that everything sole blooms before it dwindles.

Brain

For six months I've been living with Job's brain—
not the boils or righteousness, just the organ:
cut off from God, that connoisseur of pain,
who, tired of flogging Lucifer through heaven,
trussed infinite heft into a human form.
Some swear He lives; they glimpse Him in a crowd
or cancer or a poem; some feel dead
without divine fangs tearing at their id.

But our God's turned, declining to infuse
one ancient honeycomb of nerves
and one basement apartment cubicle
with something fey and subliminal
in the shivering latticework of sun,
or the winking of my PC's icon.
But it's not tricks we miss, Job's brain
and I. We miss the thought
that nothing else exists if He doesn't.

Before I rented this apartment
to live with a brain from the Old Testament,
I spent my nights groping twisted sheets.
What did I yearn for? Something in me
wanted there to be no more me,
no her, to hump two souls in one clay
until nothing was left healed,
the way God broke upon the world.

How could He think it wouldn't flow forever,
this joining that suffused pain with such pleasure
revealing in every form and syllable
a double essence. What could stay sealed?

Not rival gods. Their totems
gored creation's mystic quim,
thundering omnipotent orgasms,

receding to a muttering of dactyls.
Nor human cruelty. God fell
in among us with the repose
of a preying mantis gorging on her spouse.
And when He branded *Christ* in living flesh,
it was the feel of it He adored, the fetishes
of skin and teeth and genitals and hair,
moving through the ebb and flow of air
that was no less Him—Christ was no more
than the flayed, thorned heart of God
in a cosmic body pulsing with His blood.

Yet the garbage of this filthy garret—
the bottle caps and rubbers, peels and butts
clogging the sink where Job's cerebral matter
floats and broods—this muck appears
so unapocalyptic and inert
it must have long ago sucked out
the last molecule of grace,
drained to the gray sheen His chalice.

I slide my hands into the greasy pool
and lift and daub with a paper towel
the brain. Rancid. Bi-polar. This is God's pawn;
the prize he gave to Satan in return—
why, in return for everything: for bliss,
mortality and grief, the kiss
of transubstantiation that brings on
the shuddering that always overcomes.

The medulla oblongata quivers.
The neo-cortex, carbuncled with tumors,
shirrs while the hypothalamus
wheezes and balloons, oozing pus
that wells from the pineal gland,
the cowl of nightmare and obsession.

I lay the leaky pulp on my mattress
and lie beside it, feel its eyeless gaze
raking the stucco ceiling for a sign
that creed and intellect and rhyme
will illuminate its maker. Next life,
there will be new children, land and wife,
but tonight, our synapses still
twitch, even asleep our ventricles
burn and heave like desiccated gills.

Fathom

On the last night of my forty-seventh year
I fell to my hands and knees, immersed my head
in a spring-fed mountain pool tucked between peaks
above the volcanic moonscape of Kamchatka,
having climbed nine hours towards the blistering sun,

through elephant grass and thorns, having forded streams
and inched over granite crags, plagued by clouds
of sentient gnats and horseflies in chain mail
and mosquitoes that corkscrewed denim and wool
to suck on the writhing mass of American flesh,

and though my head sang in the freezing water,
and my knees sank to the thighs in gravelly mud,
I kissed the pool-bed moss because I knew
that I had made it alive, and that I would not fall
into a ravine, my carcass devoured by beasts,

but I knew at that moment also, raising my eyes
to squint at the snow bluing to ice between
the midnight arctic sun and the cut-glass
surface of the pool, that this was as far
into the future as I would ever walk,

though I live decades and traverse the globe,
and even as I crab-crawled down the slope
and staggered aboard a bus and pressed my cheek
against the filmy windowpane, I saw
in the blood-dark corona behind my eyes,

Petropavlovsk's trammeled thoroughfares
unfold into a skein through which I glimpsed
skylines, forests, boulevards, rivers, lakes—
the shadow print of every step I'd taken,
mapping what had threaded me this far.

And all thereafter on this Pacific cruise
a part of me stayed fixed on that Russian crest
from which my body descended on the first
dawn of my forty-eighth year to find
in every new landfall home's alembic.

Behind the slits of the ceremonial helm
of Himeji Castle's Samurai display
I glimpsed my father's eyes cowled before death.
The Maori Warriors' tongue-wild Haka dance
mimed the melodrama of first marriage.

I spent Fijian dollars in O'Sullivans,
and touched, in Australia, encrypted in the silt
belly of a hidden waterfall,
glowworms pulsing with the living code
of my children who were never born.

And always I returned to gaze at waves,
as if the ship rail I leaned over might be
the sill of my first vista. "Look," I'd shouted,
pointing my tiny fist at our new Queens
row house backyard, "Mom, look at the park!"

from **California Sonnets**

Carmel

Why do we turn away from the eternal?
Robinson Jeffers asked. The Pacific surf,
crashing against the inscape of his skull,
washed off brine and starfish, and left,
turn from the eternal. Frail vowels
spiral into the cerulean sky,
so vast it seems almost believable
there is no other we. No turning away.
I am in thrall to the inhuman voice
chanting the mantra beyond silence:
turn eternal. Drown your secret loss.
Let every moment achieve utterance.
Even the stones of Tor House mark the seconds
between the rasping slant rhymes of the ocean.

Gilroy

Waking alone at dawn today I tasted
an acrid tang in the breeze from the herb garden,
and remembered you, long forgotten,
and the day we passed the garlic festival.
We'd driven up 101 in scorching summer—
through rage, exhaustion, finally into calm,
but we did not stop for the sign that claimed
more beer per day consumed than anywhere.
Your mother (forgive, if I invoke
a name we never let you live to hear)
touched my arm, demurred;
and we drove on, for your health's sake.
It was our one parental act of love,
and you, no bigger than a clove.

Mendocino

Blunt rusted haft of abalone knife,
duct-taped, encrusted. Anglo-Saxon tongue
portending fracture, or the slipping in
between the rock face and primordial life
before the sinew clamps. In the ur-
version, I slept while hardier men
in boots and wetsuits contended against dawn
to braille-read fate in the shells' rheumy whorls.
Other texts diverge, establish
we returned triumphant, bearing meat,
to find the beach house windswept, desolate,
wives and children vanished with no trace.
I dreamt of holding fast to all I knew.
But memory's a muscle letting go.

Berkeley

I am thinking of the city of Catal Hüyük,
elder sister of Jericho, nexus
of stone-age trade, shrine of the chthonic
goddess and her fecund, polyandrous
queens. I am pondering the citizens,
innocent of wheels, of war, lovers
of cats, skilled in obsidian,
who excarnated their dead for sacred vultures.
As I walk through People's Park watching a suit
angle his head to cradle a cell phone,
I dwell on the ancient metropolis and its fate:
One day without disaster or invasion
the entire population disappeared
as if their souls were carried off by birds.

Hoops with My Junta

Any endeavor or plot involving men,
instilled by countless reps into the brain,
and calibrated until it disciplines
the air between these men—such a plan
binds all, I assert, together in a cell
codenamed, "Joy," or "Paradise," or "Soul."
Thus, the afternoon in late August '01
in an undisclosed location within
compass of waves, when six such men,
myself embedded among them,
dispersed to separate bedrooms,
re-emerged in shorts and sneakers,
to file out through the kitchen door,
and circle a pole antennaed with clematis,
I knew that for the ensuing ninety minutes
we'd play out a scenario first planted
in the deep cover of boyhood,
and even now, years after the event
that was forthcoming—of which these men,
I attest, had no presentiment—
moments on that cloudless afternoon
with heatwaves rising from macadam
and sweat glistening on tanned skin,
certain previously suspect words—
backdoor, spin, pivot, zone, reverse,
were deciphered. When the Greek
kid from Astoria head-faked,
stuck an elbow into his man's gut,
he was no longer Chief of the CIA.
No need for plausible deniability.
Lumumba linked arms with Allende,
and never did the State Department lie.
The corporate CEO pivoted
into his own shadow: a frizz-head
yelling backdoor with no budget
to spin; and me—

instead of running blind, I launched
a bomb, cheered by friends
who for ninety minutes I pretended
moored my love. Yet, I confess
that even if we could reverse
the world's spin, not one of us
six men would defect to Joy, though once
it had meant everything, if recanting
required that we be unmade, uncorking
through childhood into uninflected
nothingness. Not that we seek death,
like fanatics eyeing flight plans—as yet,
I swear, unknown—just that we want
a shimmer of towers in the distance,
and if we've lived, the committing is less
fearsome than the vaporous past,
and so we turned, when the game dissolved,
back to face the future as ourselves,
though we know we'll never land alive.

The Elsewhere

One summer solstice long ago I drove
northwest all night in the wavering
ether of highways beyond the Bronx,
rocketing past dormant satellites—
Yonkers, Hackensack, Newburgh,
approaching escape speed near Poughkeepsie,
glimpsing on dread cliffs impossible
flashes—meteors, spacecraft, even
houses perhaps breeding alien lives—
the inexorable randomness so frightening
I hurtled ever faster into the void.
Flight, yes; but no mortal pursuit—
only a fanatical faith in *hereness*
somewhere, triangulated between
accelerator and moon, a cosmic chi
exhaled as Pall-Mall smoke encoding
the energy-mass equation of *this, now*.
At last, near dawn, stars capsized,
I churned gravel coming to myself
at the double helix gate. Yaddo.
Prime Spondee. Planet of Lawn,
Honeysuckle and Turrets.
I shouldered the Ford Galaxy door open,
shielding my eyes against dilating light.
"Take two clocks and place against your ears,"
the palsied laureate declared. "Then,
separate by millions of light years."
Bench-pressing chunks of air to his tufted skull,
he grinned and rolled his eyes, then wheezed,
"Each ticks slower than the other."
This was my first dinner at the mansion
under the chandelier nebulae
and the gold-leaf firmament of the sponsoring dead,
and truth is, for days the theorem held.
Dawn's event horizon splashed my face,
led me meandering down the hall,

past candlesticks and gargoyle figurines
to my West House garret studio,
where Roth, they said, had once committed *Portnoy*.
Zodiacs scarred the massive plank desk.
The spavined couch was sticky with stale zeal.
But in my cramped head space, squinting
through quarky gloom into the blip
of a primitive curser, I caught, almost, non-
zeroness: one and one and one. At One,
inertia chuffed me out, lunchpail in fist,
to lurk in an octagon pavilion plaqued
"Donation of Helena Hampton-Smythe."
Beyond the penumbra of entwining limbs,
rhythmic thwocks and tips of a lime parabola
radared a clay tennis court where
collared white angles intersected.
Once, an aura of forsythia and star power
glided by my perch and I unswallowed,
"How's your day?" She half-turned,
eyes pooling into the middle distance,
and her lips moued as she uttered, "Bittersweet."
Then back to my capsule in the dying sun
to brood on the aqua screen until I splashed
down into paralytic nap,
deskness bonding with isotopes of drool.
Whatever mind scanned reawakening
those deep evenings: cricket gurgle,
sleep-pocked cheek, fireflies
constellating in the window box—
all coalesced just as the laureate
had prophesized: waving his fork in time,
chanting that the spaced-out mind
must pluck from thirteen strings a single
past, future and the intervals
composing all that isn't either.
Let five beats, I croaked into the moon-

lit sliver between *then* and *soon,*
monitor the frequency of *this now.*
Let this cell on this sublunary
childless tycoon's artist retreat estate
be the balloon of the expanding universe.
I inhaled ions, exhaled eons thus:
Midnight on Patrick's Bridge, I'm peering down
into the River Lee's drowned stars until
the thump of a Jersey pothole clenches my brain-
stem, triggering an El Cerrito
bar brawl which goes non-linear, plunking
the vapor trail of a little league fastball
tailing into my first, tentative
hard-on whence my father, dense
with matter, storms like a quasar
incarnating into Brooklyn,
curving space-time into a quick-
silver of humanoid history
thickening with geologic torpor,
Pangaea balled, the Antarctic
sucking Alaska's toes, morphemic soup
unrhyming into static to the always
that plancked into the dying universe.
What's more seductive than the mantra *Thnow*?
Even in the light years since those nights
it hums faint though when I crane
into the mirror and face age,
time shifts in parallax. Missing
Thnow, my lifeline hugs the shore
like a mariner bereft of longitude,
or spaceman pressing his nose to the earthward pane.
But Yaddo those first nights transmuted
particles and waves into present
sounds penetrating all. I scrolled
up and entered bold caps
cribbed from the laureate's hypnotic fork:

THE ELSEWHERE. Neither now nor when,
consequence-bereft, uncircumscribed
by past and future cones, the infinite
fraction between synapses and stars.
Out there beyond my portal, the world
stayed flat; scale insisting to the nth—
despite the post-modernist composer
scribbling all hours on the Steinway.
Summer ticked two beats past
zenith, Orion tilted declination,
and the pond thickened with crocuses and musk.
Whole days I lost, scuffling Keds
through brambly curlicues or dopplering
my Galaxy past moribund stables.
On the garlanded thoroughfare of Saratoga,
I slipped unseen among the equine
tourists preening by sleek watercolors.
In the neon-Irish sawdust-floor shebeen,
I curled into a booth sucking a pint
and stole peeks at Skidmore breasts and legs.
After a week of orbiting I finally cracked
open the oak door of the Mansion Parlor
where post-prandial junior residents
clustered around fame-fed fireballs.
"I know, out there," the Brahmin eco-
justice performance poet yawned,
stretched on a Chesterfield and gesturing
beyond the leaded glass, "Joyce and Shelley
are just a pair of Jersey cocktail waitresses...."
In a globe-lit corner, surrounded by a crown
of 18th century fauteuil, the laureate
vibrated a forefinger, declaiming,
"As Homer once said," and his voice sank,
"I'm just going to read two more...."
For all time's stringing out of space
I still, for instants, seem diverse, therefore

those evenings prism to me now, the retina
wrestling to reverse the world, transmit
into *Thnow*. But *Thnow* siphoned
into syllables no longer thrums but spins
into the singularity *As If*.
One sleepless midnight two weeks into Yaddo
I stamped up the warped stairs to my studio
and fiddled my horsehead key into the lock.
No moon, no fireflies, no stars, no sound.
I probed with splayed fingers but the string
to the unglazed lightbulb eluded and
I leaned too far and funny-boned
the phantom desk, sending dark
matter fractaling. Yipping, I slunk out,
as I slink now through another dark *As If*
melting unmeasurable hours. Next
morning, after mansion tea and scones,
I climbed to face the moonscape. Legless,
the monolith stood upended: one flank
henged the floorboards, another hewed
the window's plaster nape. A crater
loured over a spew of drafts and notes
and the crashed unblinking craft of the laptop.
Change may take epochs but it is not slow.
That morning, free from covalent bonds,
I split the couch at the vortex of smoke gyres
and surveyed—nothing. The Elsewhere
was not yet a poem; it was whatever
flowed in all directions beyond flight.
But when the clocks resynchronized
after the crash at Yaddo, The Elsewhere—
like every line graphed on this page and all
the poems encrypted through the years—
massed slowly, cooling to lambent spheres
that loom in the night sky but remain
always ineluctably somewhere else.

Reentry into dying time began
the moment I glimpsed a mildewed pad
half-buried in the rubble. Digging it out,
I unstuck the gluey weft and thumbed a text
vestigial from some ancient residence.
It lies beside me now,
this fossil from a past beyond my past,
and opening it thrills, but can't erase
distances first charted that morning
when I sat cross-legged and uncreased
abandoned couplets, haiku, axioms,
networked in a riot of vectors
esoteric as Queens subway maps.
Midway through, dog-eared, and hyped
with gargantuan violet clouds I found
THE ELSEWHERE: An Epic Beyond Rhyme.
On the next page, in miniscule block print,
If earth were made of a single atom
the nucleus would be smaller than this room.
Three more blank pages, then
the title reprised, this time wreathed in graphite
flames, spawning a new genesis
Poetry= physics, but selecting
words for a poem is just stamp-collecting.
More blanks. Then **THE ELSEWHERE** again,
enmeshed in equal signs, resulting in
Inside me mushroom 30 H-bombs.
My mouth can't even make a sound.
Throughout the rest of the composition tab
the sequence spluttered to start again and again
under the title constantly renewed
as intersecting orbits, or Greek signs.
Finally, it comet-trailed in Flair to the last draft:
I feel the presence of the past and future
but can't make The Elsewhere cohere.
And underneath, bridging a fissure

in the withered inside flap, a date
twenty-seven years before my time
above the barely legible autograph
of the man who would become the laureate.
So the last weeks passed and the residency
which began in epic flight ended with me
placing in the Yaddo ping-pong tourney
and making the rounds of Skidmore dorms.
Winched up, refurbished and rescrewed,
the great plank desk bore my elbows
groanlessly every morning and the ultra-
musty ozone of the studio
bore into my brain as lines and stanzas
millimetered forward even as far
as this but never reaching *Thnow*.
I didn't return the notebook, never spoke
to its author's incarnation as the laureate,
though zoning out during his chautauquas
or watching his knock-kneed shuffling at dusk
through the rose garden, I imagined
clocks fissioning from his ears and wondered
what he was, adrift from The Elsewhere,
wandering through Yaddo, winding down
one by one by one to nearly nought
even as the opus the world filed
under the heading *Deathless Verse*
emitted from his cloud-ringed cerebrum.
The pod I wormhole now feels absolute.
Space bears down on the winter sky
and my fingers slur over keys to enter *This
Now* even as it burgeons and
divides. Beyond, the laureate
takes his place among the planets
Shelley, *Joyce*, and *Homer* fading to
the furthest coordinate bought on Name-A-Star.
My ungloved hand counts down from five

As If Thnow could be reconciled. Before
zeroing out, I fumble to number-crunch
the hours when The Elsewhere seemed margined,
though it takes almost forever to cohere,
and an instant to extinguish, just like life.

from *To Prove My Blood: A Tale of Emigrations & the Afterlife*

Prologue. Arachne

Arachne starts with Ovid and finishes with me.
Michael Longley

Who would have thought, in 1960, when my brother's birth cramped our row house, expelling Aunt Mary back to Brooklyn, that a fat slice of the century later hers would be the last penny the McCanns would spend? Brooklyn should have made a quick end to her, but she flourished. At the age of sixty-one, Mary Martin began a career as a cleaning lady at the Borough Hall Board of Education, clanking through plaster labyrinths, shouldering fire doors, palming ashtrays, and single-handedly reviving the myth of an era when every brownstone boasted its Irish maid.

"Hey, Mary," the suits would tease, as she flicked her dust mop through olive cubicles, "You're doing a great job there. Rubbing like you're going to conjure a genie."

"Show me the bottle, Gorgeous," she'd rattle back. "It would take that baldy fella to clean your dirt."

She had them on a string—the psychologists and specialists, the social workers and the Ph.D.s. Everyone turned to her for proof that a primeval Brooklyn still shadowed.

And in September 1966, when my brother toddled off to St. Kevin's first-grade, even my mother turned to Mary. Alone all day, my mother felt our six rooms shrink to the size of bouillon cubes. The rut she dug to drain off entropy—a wash, a sweat with Jack LaLane, a smoke with tea—soon sludged with livid waste. She tippled, she waked her girlhood, and finally, her nerves stretched until she had to scream or flee.

I was eleven, used to the phone calls my mother made to Brooklyn nightly since Mary'd been packed off, how she'd climb the stairs, sit cross-legged on the bed and light a cigarette, cradling the receiver in the crook of her neck. Sometimes I'd trail after her, badgering about school or toys, while Mary's voice, amped by Ma Bell, poured into her other ear.

"I had the toast, y'know," she'd sing. "The rye toast, at the Meyer's Deli. The bread's gorgeous. There's a new man at the counter. A new Jewish man, with the quiff and the funny hat, y'know. At the counter. A terrible hum coming off his greatcoat, Pet, like mousy cheese!"

"That's nice, Mary, and did you shop today?"

"Not a bit of it. Well, I was at the Woolworth's, y'know, on Grand Street, with the dollar sign. 'Tis dear, Pet, the Woolworth's is, disgraceful, shag the coupons, and Pet, you can't tell boys from girls with the nests of hair...."

But one night, my mother broke through, wrangled the old woman from her litany of chores and toast, and stirred a memory of childhood when Mary had fed and washed her baby sister, her Pet, twenty years her junior. How, I don't know. But whatever prayer she uttered, it was heard, and it set Mary spinning her one plot: to save her sister by bringing her back to Brooklyn.

"A rare thing, a quare talent altogether," Mary hummed, fiddling her brush over the braided yarmulke of Dr. Rosenshein. "It's in the fingers, you see, Doctor. She's always had it."

Her wenned hands fluttered in another world, inches from his beard. "Why, she taps letters the way Paderewski plays piano. And a smile like my Pet's! She'd be the best secretary in the world."

And so Anne Brady, née McCann, youngest of four girls ferried from Ulster in 1922, dubbed "Pet" in the ur-time of Brooklyn, followed her eldest sister on their youthward journey over the Kosciusko Bridge. She made a great success (her smile demonstrating the required teeth) and was appointed clerk at Borough Hall, where her touted fingers dipped into the pork barrel her sister had pried open.

But it didn't stop there. One evening at the dinner table a month after my mother started her new job, my father announced that he'd been fingered for something big. He was leaving the Police Force to be top bird for a new Fingerprint Security System at 110 Livingstone Street in the Brooklyn Borough Hall Board of Education. He winked at his stunned fiefdom, swiping his martini over the meatloaf. The matter was being considered. It was being handled personally by a nabob at the Board of Ed., a gentleman by the name of Dr. Joel S. Rosenshein.

Did my father trace his apotheosis to Aunt Mary? Did he suspect that returning her to Brooklyn from her seat in the parlor wingback of 53-28 194th Street, Flushing, precipitated a kind of continental drifting, leading inexorably toward me, toward what I'm left with now, in Ohio, childless, the rain lashing outside and a great bare oak rising from the earth in a frozen rage of limbs?

It was his job to trace, but anyone sheathed in flesh for very long begins to sense that some clues need to be processed by a special organ, an internal reality filter stuck in there somewhere between chakras, and in my father this organ was as tough as a boxing glove and strong enough to metabolize whole fifths of lethal facts.

But for all his fantasies, his swagger, his limericks, and his garlanded swivel chair in the Borough Hall Board of Education, it's not him, and not his wife, and none of the litter of Eumenides begotten to Ulster and spirited west by Francis and Sarah McCann, but only the eldest, Mary Martin, who's survived.

She's still here, living in a nursing home down the street from me, eking the last few moments from the century whose first light spawned her. And though she's dwindled to a nerveless thing, shriven of memory, in the afternoons she taps her foot softly on her wheelchair's pad, as if warming to an antediluvian reel.

And though the four McCann girls propagated diligently with their share of the navvies, lollards, cops, and narrowbacks of Irish Brooklyn, mine is the only shadow clinging to the last quicksilver of a breathing dream. I'm the only one enwebbed in myth, craving to spin and also to break free, to make and to make up. And what is it I would spin or break? What's flesh anyway, especially to me, whose office is to watch its arachnid shriveling? Maybe it's death I have to spin out of myself—out of my fear, my craving. Maybe these words offer the only hope for Mary Martin née McCann to start the long swim back through time.

Chapter 2. Wave & Particle

God keep me from knowledge of myself.
—Rachel Korn

Mary may exist in the myth-wave, but on Sundays, when I wheel her out
of the nursing home, pack her into my car, and drive the few blocks to my
apartment, she feels like a weighty particle. She is the joint's ache, what can't
be hugged, what can't vault out of herself or melt into the crazy quilt's soft
warmth. When I touch her doughy wrist, I feel the origin of the tear between
myth and time, wave and particle, as in the buckle of a root-stressed sidewalk.
She jolts, wails "Ma!" and I lift her by the armpits, hugging her bulbous torso,
and struggle around the coffee table, through the foyer, into the bathroom,
where I unfiddle her nylons and peel the viscous panties. I dab her stout thighs
with a nest of Kleenex, and mop a trail through the grottiness of Mary Martin,
then we waltz to the couch, and I plop her down and unstop a half-bucket of
Dewars to water my parched cells. And a thimbleful to quicken Mary's nerves,
whatever wave they dream in. In what's called me, in what's called her, that
potion is deadening, livening right now. God grant we don't outlive ourselves,
and a safe journey.

Inside Mary Martin there is still a myth she wakens from, dangling from any
of its tines: posing at a booth in Schraft's with her mother and sisters flaunting
pillbox Easter hats; Mary eyes the bassinet of salt sticks; the Times Square
neon news-ticker undulates DUNKIRK. Then she dives into sleep, reemerges
in 1917 palming a shilling at the counter of McCray's Tobacconist and Hair-
dresser on Merchants Quay. She's seventeen: the Brits, the blackened husks
of buildings, the wailing mothers crowd just beyond her ken in a future she
escaped; but her young breasts smelling of loam and soap, her calves matted
with fine hair—they are waiting to embody dream: What should she buy? She
wakes on a couch in her nephew's living room in Ohio; she screams "Ma!" in a
senility so perfect it floods the brain, braiding wave and particle.

But like anything else, senility requires toil. In my forties, my waist softening
despite drill and starvation, I can only imagine the effort it must take Mary
Martin, without stationary bike or vim pills, to perfect memory. Once sleep
was her praxis, and she thrashed nightly on the swayback palette of her Brooklyn
flat; but no matter how hard she labored to make dream and time cohere, when

she woke up, she was always sealed in that sixty-or seventy-or eighty-or ninety-year-old body. Sunlight filtered through the lace over the dresser. She gripped the coverlet and breathed, while the sepia dream dissolved. Years of spindling rounds at Borough Hall, pursefuls of quarters pushed through Automat slots, wave after wave of Welkian bubbles, monthly Rosary Society bus trips to the Cloisters, and always the nightly phone call from Queens finally induced in Mary a satori of entropy, until she was able to unify the fields while still awake, to slip out of her flat, past the thrice-locked door, to glide through decades and continents without so much as twitching an eye.

Now her discipline is so keen that she *is* the myth, the wave, the waking particle and dream. But all I hear at my desk, as I stare out the window at a shivering oak, is a lick of sibilance burbling from unguessed depths. It sounds like this:

Son, do you remember the time, the time it is, do you remember, son, the time and is it this, the time that you remember? Do you remember that? Son, do you like to drive? Do you drive, son? It's gorgeous, the drive to Hempstead, the long drive. I'm fine, son, I'm grand so, and I'm fine, your mother's gone, gone now, and I wasn't allowed out without her, on dates even, I wasn't allowed.

Chapter 9. Wiretap

> I am walking backward into the future like a Greek.
> —Michael Longley

When I was growing up, the denizens of Queens walked like Dante's sodomites: heads and feet cranked arsewards. Everyone went both ways, baleful gazes aiming westward toward Manhattan's hordes, nipples stiffened toward the prefab nirvana of Long Island.

The fear and desire that unscrewed my head and cranked it around was Father. My own first, but not just him: there was Monsignor Barry, the martinet who drilled altar boys in liturgical Latin; and later, Jack Sullivan, crew-cut maniac coach of Fordham Prep, who'd skip full-jacketed into the shower for hugs. I puppied after teachers, jocks, movie stars, anything with a codpiece.

It is possible to travel a long way so contorted. Last year, my breastbone pointed toward the seacoast of West Cork and my head screwed backward toward the cottage where the latest incarnation of my father, a famous poet, one of the Cork crow-robes, ate his lunch.

In 1975, it had taken three day's nerve to mount the stairs to his office. Taking a breath, I'd knocked and, hearing a muffled grunt, turned the knob and entered the dim, musty sanctum crammed with books. Pictures hung askew—an inked Joyce, a chieftain's death mask. On the bare floorboards sat a desk spavined with tomes, and behind, silhouetted in twilight, roosted the poet, his Norman head with its crest of white hair floating above the turtleneck of a fisherman's knit sweater. His eyes were recessed deep under his brow, and tiny blue deltas marked his ruddy cheeks.

Opening a fist whose swan ring spread over two knuckles, he seated me, and after a few sweating clock-ticks I blurted that he and I came from the same neighborhood, then gushed a line of one of his poems I'd learned rocking at the cabinet hi-fi. The poet canted his aquiline nose and, sidestepping my faux pas, asked how well I knew Brooklyn, where he'd spent childhood years before returning to Ireland.

"My parents," I confessed.

He swiveled toward the tiny window, and sighing, said it was past time. I jumped to my feet, pivoted to the door, but he continued, "Past time for a pint, isn't it?"

"Yes, if you mean, I mean, that's great," I stammered.

He led me down the stairs and out into the wind of Western Road, and we matched strides past the Lee eddy with its green phone booth, past Fr. Matthew's statue and the Patrick Street Cinema featuring *Jaws*, down the alley of Oliver Plunkett Street, and into the musky warmth of the Long Valley, a tiled barroom with Tiffany lamps and trays of crustless sandwiches and radishes and celery stalks and slabs of soda bread. The poet wended through the late-afternoon crowd and seated himself at an oval stone-heavy table, beckoning the two Murphy's pints the barman had brought unbidden. With a pencil tweezed from his breast pocket, he nibbed dashes and question marks in the margins of the poem I'd pressed on him, all the while humming to the barman's flow of chatter about Hitler's private life. And so the night slid by—a blur of pints and faces—students, fans, dossers, and prognosticators dropping by to spar with the poet and check out the Yank.

"It's an arid place for the spirit, the States is," said one curly-haired youth with granny glasses and a red-and-white tasseled scarf, stinging me into a paean to Robert Bly, the Great Mother Goddess conference, yoga retreats, astrology, and free love.

Twitching an eyebrow, the poet said, "I wonder if Bly isn't just a mad Protestant farmer."

He knew everyone on both sides—Berryman and Lowell and Williams and Roethke and Kavanagh and Gogarty and Clarke and Beckett. He'd shared poteen with Behan and tea with Mrs. Yeats and fly-fished with Ted Hughes and crossed the Bay Bridge on the back of Gary Snyder's motorcycle, and he gossiped as if they were a pack of quarrelsome neighbors. It was the first of many magical evenings, ending with weak-kneed ambles through the sleeping city to Tivoli in mist that always seemed wetter than American rain.

Over the years, I tracked his zigzagging from Albany to Cork to San Francisco to Pittsburgh, and when I'd spot him I'd elbow through the small throng of hangers-on, unfolding my newest aspirations, which, if I got him alone, he would chevron with arabesques, humming, slinging koans.

"Who are your contemporaries?" he asked once, making me think of my struggling school friends, all of us angling for a passport to Parnassus. And I remember the searching look he gave me when he said, "Every poet has a secret wound."

After a gala reading at the 92nd Street Y in New York, he bunked the night at 53-28, and that evening Phil Brady chauffeured us on one of his city tours, cruising through Queens pointing out the locations of famous benders, mob deals, and shoot-outs. After one spine-tingling swerve around a traffic snarl, we ended up at Peter Luger's steak house in Brooklyn, with its charred rafters and creamed spinach and waiters looking like refugees from the Luftwaffe. My heart still pounding from the near-accident, I darted glances from father to father as they traded tales of politicos, crooks, and gunmen as exotic as Gods and Fighting Men. I realized that the poet wouldn't have to ask about my wound.

That's how I came last year to be guest, cook, and driving instructor at the cottage where he spent months each year with Mia, a black-haired pixie from Sarah Lawrence, younger than I was. I picked my way over the sheep-dipped gorse into the kitchen, where the pair bent over the deal table, spooning bowls of my stew.

"Not bad," the poet lied.

I shrugged, tossed a wreath of keys onto the table, and said, "Let's take a spin."

We crossed the path to the antique Ibuzu I'd bought from the local garage, and I folded my legs into the right side, forgetting that everything here is backward. My pupils watched me slide into the death seat then climbed in after, and as the poet worried the stick shift, I palmed his hand, saying, "It's easy, remember? Down first, then over. And gentle with the clutch." I thought of quoting his lines, "changing gears with/ the same gesture as/ eased your snowbound/ heart and flesh," but, remembering my gaffe on the day we first met, I bit my tongue.

"Reverse, you bastard," the poet said, and the buggy spasmed backward, scattering sheep.

Over Mount Gabriel we threaded unshouldered paths to Schull, a small crescent inlet of the sea, where we lurched to a stop and disembarked, light-headed, for an afternoon pint. Soon we were safely squatting on three-legged stools by a turf fire.

"To luck," I lifted my glass, "we'll need it to cross back over that mountain."

"We barely outran our shadow," the poet scoffed. "New York's where the real slaughter goes on," he turned to his girlfriend and described how my father, one finger on the wheel, had driven us through the back streets of Brooklyn, pointing out scenes of obscure calumny. The tour and our lives almost ended when my father drifted in mid-sentence through a stop sign into boulevard traffic.

"If that's how you learned to drive," Mia said, "what kind of murderers will you make of us?"

The barman, a giant with a reckless black beard, brought us our pints and disappeared into the lounge. Leaning in conspiratorially, the poet whispered, "This is Bailey's local, you know." I took in the small stone room, pewter mugs on the mantle, a lacquered oar and harpoon displayed on the wall. "Is that why it's empty?" I asked.

These days the mention of Ian Bailey stirred murmurs even in empty rooms. He was one of the army of "blow-ins" who swarmed into West Cork seeking a haven, wayfarers of all stripes, from Tony Blair and Jeremy Irons, whose summer homes were nestled under the shadow of Mount Gabriel, all the way down to the Austrian palm-reader who ran a tea shop in Ballydehob and the paparazzi who retired from chasing Princess Di to do photo shoots of "Writers on Bicycles." The local grocery store was run by Oregon hippies; yoga seminars were advertised on pub doors.

An aspiring poet and journalist, Bailey had come from Liverpool to West Cork, took up the bodhrán, Hibernicized his name to Eoin O'Baille, hired out as gardener to the poet, and, like so many of us, slipped his verses under the poet's pencil. But all his aspirations had darkened one morning six months before, when the body of Sophie Toscan du Plantier, a beautiful thirty-nine-year-old French woman, wife of a French film producer, was discovered lying a hundred feet from her holiday home in Toormoor, near Schull. It was Bailey, working as a stringer for the Cork Examiner, who'd broken the story, and his intimate knowledge of the crime scene raised questions about the nature of his source. The victim's skull had been smashed with a blunt instrument—a club or hammer, he'd reported. There'd been no sign of robbery or sexual assault, and the Gardai wondered if the assailant was known by the victim; who else but a neighbor or acquaintance would be let in so late at night? Rumors swirled that an opened bottle of wine and two washed glasses had been found on the kitchen table. There were whispers that Bailey had confessed, saying, "I went too far." The only other suspect was a German businessman who committed suicide, leaving a note that vaguely implicated him in "something bad." But nothing could be proved, and though the Gardai had arrested Bailey twice, both times they'd released him, to the chagrin of the French government, which saw the botched investigation as an international affront.

Anywhere else this might have been stale news, but here, just a few miles from the spot where Michael Collins had been ambushed, politics had always been the main motive for killing. The poet's eyes glinted with intrigue. Was it a failed love affair? Attempted rape?

"It could have been anyone," he said. "West Cork's swarming with sex mechanics."

"Listen," I said, "why don't I go see Bailey. I have my father's badge. I'll tell him I'm a New York cop brought here to consult. He wants to be a journalist. Here's his chance."

"You gobshite," the poet snorted. "Don't you know everyone already knows who you are. You can't wipe your arse around here without the world and his brother holding his nose."

And so, as the bar darkened, the talk having turned to murder, I slipped a poem out of my jacket pocket and asked the poet if he wouldn't take a look.

"It's about my father," I said. "It's a few years old. About the Crimmins case. I've been reworking it."

"The poem or the murder?" he asked, as he patted his vest for a pencil. "You haven't heard about this, I think, my dear. Tell Mia about Alice." The poet took a sturdy pull on his pint and scraped his stool to the fire as I told my fellow New Yorker about my father's case.

One August evening, midway between World War Two and now, my brother and I were called in from the amniotic air of 194th Street and scrubbed and swatted upstairs. The vacuum roared; the liquor cabinet drawbridged to reveal emerald and gold bottles; polished ashtrays garnished the end tables. Tonight, coming for cocktails: Alice Crimmins, whose picture was blazoned on the front page of the Daily News, looking like Jackie Kennedy with scarf and sunglasses.

Alice lived the life that was not admitted to exist in Queens. She had affairs and drank bourbon in low-life bars. She divorced, remarried the same man, divorced him again. She faced straight ahead, didn't swerve around priest or cop. Maybe that's why she wore sunglasses at night. When her children went missing on the night of June 23, it didn't take the detectives long to point fingers. Though there were no witnesses and no physical evidence, though the first detective on the scene botched the crime-scene photos, though Alice had no conceivable motive to murder her children, the investigation torqued down on her. The evidence: the men, the booze, the sunglasses.

"If she was my wife, I'd kill her," one dick growled. But they only had to break her, and they set about grilling her at the precinct, buttonholing her boyfriends, harassing the offices where she did temp work under an assumed name. Her estranged husband they dismissed as a fool and cuckold without brains or guts enough to govern his wife, much less kill his children.

On the day, two weeks after the disappearance, when they found the missing girl under a hedge near the old World's Fair site, they brought Alice to identify the decaying corpse without warning her about what she was about to see. She fainted on the spot—more proof of guilt—the theatrical ploy, when she'd shown no grief till then. During the months that followed, she continued to drink and dance and lure men back to her Kew Gardens apartment: a Mafioso, a Long Island real estate shark, even a cop. Guilty, guilty, guilty. But how prove it?

So they brought in Phil Brady: plaid-lapelled, purse-lipped, with a priest's bearing, peacock pheromones and a voice that fluttered the hearts of waitresses. Though he was a CYO coach, Holy Name bigwig, and church usher, head cranked back to the Catholic fantasy of Queens, nose listing to port, there was, inside his florid body, an emerald that changed hue, emanating from each facet a different mood.

Because of his MP technical experience, eavesdropping from Normandy to Bohemia, he was called into the Alice Crimmins case not to investigate but to listen, assigned to wiretap Alice's apartment, her car, the booth in her local tavern. He sat in a dark van listening to her lovemaking, her weeping, her cursing. This was his gift, a gift I never knew he had: to listen, to absorb the confessions of others and remain himself. Though the Alice Crimmins case spun the heads of the NYPD, there was a place inside Phil Brady that nobody was going to touch.

That August night when Alice Crimmins rang the doorbell, I sneaked out of bed and crawled to the top of the stairs to glimpse between the banister rails the famed murderess in a flame cocktail dress, highball in one hand, cigarette in the other, laughing and talking, sitting cross-legged on the couch. My father was hunched forward, my mother perched in her orange Queen Anne chair, swinging her crossed leg in time to the Mitch Miller LP playing on the hi-fi, and suddenly, I felt the weather change. Alice shrank into herself, her beehive bobbing with cramped sobs. My mother's leg froze; my father rose from his recliner and glided like a bearish cloud to the couch. Whispering, he draped his huge arm over her shoulder. I'd never seen him hold my mother the way he held Alice that night, and she sobbing and sobbing.

What I didn't learn until years later, when I read *The Alice Crimmins Case*, is that our basement had been as carefully prepared for Alice's visit as the rest of the house. There, amid the flotsam of unmatched socks and old trophies, three detectives hunkered over a massive tape recorder. What could they have made of what they heard—a scratchy voice whispering, "There, there?" A woman's sobs? Maybe the hidden mikes were sensitive enough to catch the pounding of a child's heart.

Telling the story in a quiet pub in the penumbra of another murder, I conjured Alice Crimmins, Goddess, mounting the stairs quietly to my childhood.

"How did it end?" Mia asked.

"She was convicted, finally, after two trials. Served eight years. I heard that she moved to Florida when she got out. She'd be in her eighties now, if she's alive."

"Did you write this before your father died?" the poet asked, having turned back to us now, his glass empty.

"Yes."

"Did you show him?"

"All he said was, 'you got some facts wrong.' Nothing about the poem—about him and me and how I couldn't ever say what I needed to."

"Maybe he was afraid," the poet said.

"It was me who was afraid." I said. "Not to die—I didn't even squeak in the backseat when he nearly killed us, remember? I was afraid to face. . . ."

"Face what?"

I had no answer. The barman had slipped back in, and watching him glance at us sidelong, I thought of Ian Bailey, who'd once frequented this bar, having come to Ireland yearning for a home he'd never known. Was it his specter that paralyzed me? His words, stammered, revised, submitted to a poet, swallowed, finally congealed into a hammer propelled by madness. I knew his failure. Was I terrified of walking mute and outlawed in his shoes?

My father taught me everything except this: to converse with a Goddess and still keep a place inside that stays untouched. And my father, in the guise of an Irish poet, slid my poem, marked with his cuneiform, across the table, saying, "You might make something of this."

Meaning not, as Phil Brady would have meant, a life. Meaning, I hope, a filament entwining words and world.

"Enough blather. Let's hear the poem," the poet said.

Wiretap

How could Detective Brady and his perky wife
storm upstairs to enforce lights out
when the blonde cross-legged on their sofa
had strangled her two children?
                                            Perfectly safe,
I moled between the two top banister rails,
Eavesdropped a spill, a laugh, and something clicking.
She must have sloshed her cocktail,
slipped her heels off. Soon,
muffled sobs, my father's tenor voice, *there there*.
Unthinkable now to slink back to my room,
dream murder mounting the pillowy stairs barefoot.
Maybe the girl puked up the night of June 23
or the boy sassed—maybe it was finally
too much—the late night waitressing, the boyfriends,
divorce in Queens in 1965.
Unthinkable—solitude a thing I couldn't bear—
still is—internal voices whisper *home*
and twice they've nearly had me married.
The cops had Alice's Ford or something close
reliably witnessed cruising 3:30 AM.
Next day, they chalked one tiny corpse near Kew Gardens.
The other—the girl—nested in the weeds
of the World's Fair for two weeks.
Once a year, when my father picks me up at Kennedy,
we pass the silver skeleton Fair globe
without a word for that grim search,
the Crimmins trial—the sentence long since passed.
Although his Queens is a kind of wax museum
(at this gin mill Fuentes outbled Diaz,
at this ristorante Anthony Grace fell)
his famous case—the one they made a book—
this one he hates, because, he says,
my mother is not "perky"and some facts are fudged.
True, as the book says, mick bloodhounds
were bent on nailing that bitch Crimmins—

their eyes glazed over when she claimed
she checked the sleeping kids at 3 o'clock.
Instead, they teased clues from her beehive hairdo,
they sleuthed right through the shades
she donned for Daily News splash pics.
Kelly was stone stubborn, Pierig horny
to make second grade. They had the car,
they had the coroner pinning the first death
near 2 A.M. Still, they needed a mole—
someone they trusted, someone she would trust.

In *The Alice Crimmins Case,*
Detective Brady's manner is "confessional"—
and after twenty years, a heart attack,
cancer and four strokes, still is.
Clasping his hands, he hoods the dinner table
and the fact I am a liberal atheist
exudes from me like sweat
but never does the conversation stray
as far as who he is.
                              Mention the Crimmins case
and something inside him clicks,
something is welled in echoes,
something behind his eyes begins to spin
like the reel to reel that hunkered on his desk,
state of the art, 1965. I grew up
too busy jerking off and freebasing
pure heresy at Fordham Prep
to eavesdrop cop tapes, but last month,
years after I stormed out the 53-28
screen door swearing new life, I spied,
wedged on a lost shelf in the basement
of a Berkeley used book shop, the familiar
discounted title. Sobs welled up
in that California cellar, most distant point
in the farthest orbit around Queens I'd dared,

so far I feared that if I took two steps,
nothing would pull back.

Yet, thumbing that pulp, I realized
my father had traveled farther.

What did it mean in 1965
to tape those sobs, then turn his back
on Kelly and Pierig, press erase?
Queens was a world honeycombed with generations,
a safe place for white men and most women.
What did it take to replay for the defense
proof the coroner fudged time of death?
The hack who wrote *The Alice Crimmins Case*
and juiced those sobs to hawk his schlock exposé
invents "two sleepless nights" for Detective Brady
before he wakes Alice's sad sack lawyer.
But when I think of that ineffectual,
or just imaginary phone call,
I see a door open and my father
take two steps into nothing—
but for all my traveling, I'll never know—
and though I want him not to go on
being him, me being me,
I haven't stopped, nor found a way
to tell all this to anyone I love.

from *Phantom Signs: The Muse in Universe City*

The Man of Double Deed

Being childless, my childhood has receded into myth.

I must have had parents and schlepped to school and played games and wept and laughed and yawned through Sunday Mass. But what I remember best is rocking in front of the family hi-fi. All afternoon, back and forth, I rocked to Father's scratchy Clancy Brothers albums. Goddesses and tinkers and book-wrights and spirit eels and the hated Sassenach and the hosting of the Sidhe—all hissed and babbled through the needled grooves. No words, only utterance. On hands and knees, speed adjusted to song, I soared over the streets. My heels kept me from regressing beyond Queens, but I embodied an oceanic voyage, finding in rhythm a charm against time's surge.

Rocking in front of the cabinet hi-fi I first heard the man of double deed. He made no sense. He befuddled all the senses, and he still does. He doubles and twists and dervishes. His seed becomes snow becomes birds becomes ship becomes stick becomes knife.

When I ask him, "Why don't I remember any words but yours?" the man of double deed croons, "Like birds lose words inside of song."

I have never seen the man of double deed. But I have heard him many times in my own voice.

"Let me sing him once," I say. "And you'll have him by heart."

No one—not playground of third graders, nor clutch of drunks, nor pride of grad students, nor sailors nor hedge funders nor inmates nor rest-home dwellers—has ever heard him twice, or needed to. No one has failed, after one hearing, to forget everything but the man of double deed.

At first they doubt.

"How can we know him after just one time?"

Then silence ripples, and the listening approaches the intensity of the moment before a thunderstorm.

The man of double deed enters the air. He is here and beyond. He is heard. Sometimes my arms join in and fingers peck to sow the seed, and dance in the air as the seed turns to a garden full of snow, and my hands flit like birds upon a wall and drift up turning to a shipwreck in the sky and whip down like a stick upon my back and finally clench a fist to plunge a penknife into my heart. And I am dead and dead indeed.

But I can't write him down. I might break the spell. I might lose him forever, the way Homer lost utterance when he learned to write.

When the famous Homer scholar Milman Parry asked an unlettered bard if it was possible to remember a nightlong poem after just one hearing, the bard nodded.

"Word for word?"

"Word for word."

The next night the bard spoke the poem, and Parry recorded it and compared it to the night before and it was the same poem but with completely different words. Like birds he lost the words inside of song. But when the bard learned to write, he created an original outside himself and lost the ability to compose. No longer could lines be conceived and spoken in one breath. Time and myth were cleaved. The light was silenced.

What's a word if it isn't written down? Until the alphabet locks them down in time, words are breath. They generate themselves. They are like William Matthews's waves—not water but a force that water welcomes and displays. Because he is not written, the man of double deed welcomes and displays all utterance, including several species of the dead indeed.

No one hears the man of double deed the same way, but two things always happen.

First, "Like birds it was upon the wall" always changes to "It was like birds upon the wall."

I have come to believe that my birds—they of the syntactic inversion—are a late interpolation, crafted by the children of Homer to exploit the dynamics of the alphabet. Acrobats of syntax are Homer's children, sleight-of-handers who know that the line gains strength by avoiding opening with three weak syllables. Homer's progeny love drama. "Like birds," they say, and for an instant the reader tingles with conflict and possibility.

But those who hear the man of double deed just once are not listening to anyone. They are raptured in cadence and the transubstantiation from early snow to late birds. They feel a force that language welcomes and displays.

It was like birds upon the wall.

The second thing is the shipwreck in the sky. Here, all the voices—the one in the back row and the one drooling on the bar and the one too cool for school and the one who hasn't really heard—all chorus together.

'Twas like a shipwreck in the sky. Of the seven images, this is the most striking. When all chime in on the sky shipwreck, I know that although we rock in time with the surf, we still adore the phantasmagorical world. The birds of aural imagination and the ship of visual imagination are both engaged. The man of double deed lives in both species. There is sound inside the light.

In his noble introduction to Fagles's *Iliad*, Bernard Knox says that each of Homer's dactylic hexameter lines displays the arrangement of the whole poem. Each begins with conflict and possibility, and proceeds through a variety of sounds to fill the metrical requirements. But each line ends with the same strict pairing of dactyl and spondee. The poem is inside each line—from possibility to finality. By the end of the *Iliad*, the force of the story has been welcomed and displayed sixteen thousand times.

The man of double deed is not sixteen thousand lines, he is fourteen—or so I imagine, since I've never counted. But he has been recited so many times now in so many versions that perhaps he nears sixteen thousand lines. How many knives have pricked his heart? How many deaths has he suffered or, perhaps, forestalled?

Once, a surgeon stuck a penknife in my heart and I was dead, but not indeed. There was sound inside the light. I was wheeled in and instead of counting down I recited the man of double deed. He sang that I was dead indeed which meant I would not be dead, since rhythm is a charm against time's surge.

Had I passed completely into myth, I might have recited all of Homer after one hearing.

"How do you remember all those words?" Charon would have asked.

"Like birds lose words inside of song," I'd have sung, rocking back and forth in his sky shipwreck.

I wasn't dead indeed but I was intubated for an eon and could sing only imaginary songs. So, Tuesday evenings from June till March, birds gathered upon a wall and since the man of double deed was too short, we migrated all the way from Stately Plump Buck Mulligan to Yes I said Yes I will Yes.

None was dead indeed or transcendent or even adept, so we required an outward sign. We needed one printed copy of *Ulysses*, in all its editorially disputed leaves. But because we never saw the man of double deed and because Homer never saw the *Iliad* and because Joyce was so blind he could hardly see Sylvia Beach, we shared just the one codex. We sowed the book until it turned to snow. One bird read. Then another, while the flock listened.

We listened for the sound inside the light. We listened until we heard the force *Ulysses* welcomes and displays.

Every Tuesday night two things happened.

First, Dublin and Ithaca crashed like a shipwreck in the sky.

Second, we heard what wasn't written: possibility and conflict yielding to illuminated sound.

Yes I said Yes I will Yes. Yes I said Yes I will Yes.

We heard it when it wasn't said. We heard it when it was.

It was a thrum beneath each unlineated line.

The final dactyl of the *Iliad* is "tamer of horses." In the *Odyssey*, "form and voice." *Ulysses's* final utterance is "yes." With each new version, matter is doubled more fully into sound.

One Tuesday night a form and voice came from beyond the sky-wrecked dactyls, and I stepped out into the blindfolded night and there she was on the doorstep, sitting on her haunches: Molly Bloom.

She regarded me. I regarded her.

She was outside human ken until she spoke—the same syllable as her first utterance as Calypso. "Mn," she said, and stepped, tail high, into her name.

The closest I come to seeing the man of double deed is when I regard Molly Bloom from a distance of ten paces. We regard each other, pharaohically.

"What transpires, Molly?" I inquire.

Sometimes her ears turn toward the query and sometimes they do not.

Is she further than my childhood? Farther than Homer? Is she farther than the place I go to hear the man of double deed?

For all her fecund lexicon, Molly Bloom's first utterance as Calypso is still the one I hear when I regard our Molly: "Mn."

It is the sound missing from the last word I heard on the operating table. Its absence was the reason I wasn't dead indeed.

The surgeon who penknifed Joyce's heart is Stately Plump Buck Mulligan.

"Ah the Greeks, Dedalus," he intones. "You must read the original."

Dedalus trembles. Even the sea, in the original, is fearsome: snot-green, scrotum-tightening. But Homer had no original. *Ulysses* has hundreds of originals. Just ask Darantiere, the printer.

If you forget the words, remember song, and the world unfolds whole in every line. This is the force welcomed and displayed in the months I came back to life.

Humans do not own speech, even when we inscribe it. The page does not define words. Beneath Joyce's sentences are measures. Though he wrote thirty thousand different words, each contained what was not written down: the sleep inside the waking, the sound inside the light, the *mn* inside the deed.

Yes I said Yes I will Yes.

My childhood is myth, but Molly Bloom continues to take form and voice. She has been Calypso. She has been Penelope. She has been a calico cat. Today she is a five-year-old girl. Her given name is Mia. I introduced her father to the man of double deed and he passed him on to his young daughter. She heard him once, knew him right away, and made him hers, word for word.

Here is Mia's Man of Double Deed

> There is a man of double deed.
> He's in his garden sowing seeds.
>
> When the seeds began to grow
> 'Twas like a garden full of snow.
>
> When the snow began to melt
> It was like a ship without a bell.
>
> When the ship began to sail,
> It was like a bird without a tale.
>
> When the bird began to fly,
> It was like an eagle in the sky.
>
> When the sky began to roar
> 'Twas like a lion at my door.
>
> When my door began to crack
> 'Twas like a stick upon my back
>
> When my back began to smart
> 'Twas like a penknife in my heart.
>
> When my heart began to bleed,
> It was death, death, death indeed.

Those who fear the man of double deed fear the original. Homer had no original, and Joyce knew no Greek, and Mia has no fear. She has heard the force which the poem welcomes and displays. Her bird has no tale. Her Molly is a lion. She has spun the sound inside the light. She is *mn*.

Mia has released me from the spell. Now I can regard the man of double deed, knowing that this is only one version, only now and mine, and no original.

Here he is, as he was when I rocked in front of the hi-fi.

> There was a man of double deed
> Who sowed his garden full of seed.
>
> When the seed began to grow
> 'Twas like a garden full of snow.
>
> When the snow began to fall
> Like birds it was upon the wall.
>
> When the birds began to fly
> 'Twas like a shipwreck in the sky.
>
> When the sky began to crack
> 'Twas like a stick upon my back.
>
> When my back began to smart
> 'Twas like a penknife in my heart.
>
> And when my heart began to bleed
> Then I was dead and dead indeed.

Now close your eyes and rock. Meet him yourself.

from *Forged Correspondences*

Hunger's Painting

Safe
        returned to America
some days I stare
        so long across the room
at a sand painting
        sketched on a maize sack
and framed for souvenir

I can almost see
        beneath its gaudy outline
of African lake and sky
        a lake floor
far below
        on fire

Black mud coughs
        watery blue flames
behind the pastel scene
        of fishing boats
and eucalyptus
        that hangs on my office wall

Hunger painted it
        and shadowed me down
mud paths past
        palm oil mamas and
pans of matchstick-tiny *ndakala* fish
        past soldiers squatting on their helmets
and the sassy malachite smuggler
        in Chicago White Sox T-shirt—

Hunger
        a tall man
in green *abas-cost*
        and ragged polyester shorts
hawked the dream sketch
        still damp

pinching my sleeve
        to coax *monsieur l'americain*

Now
        daily for me
the Kamalondo *marché*
opens:
        bundles of ghost
papaya, squash, and mangoes
        blister into flame

while children waft after toy wire cars
        and zip sparks down the leads
to melt the skeleton frames

In the rich
        wet smoke of the *Gécamines*
miners are finally freed

        by drowning

No one can check
        company boots doled out
or pints of milk
        gulped at the mouth
of the mine to protect bone

I spend whole days
        fascinated
                staring

The jacarandas
        lining the pitted dirt roads
crinkle like paper maché
        the bullet-pocked buildings
                undulate in flames

At night in the bodegas
              batik *pagnes*
of dancers rouged with fever
              swirl
eerie as manta rays
              to reveal
fiery helix of muscle scorching thigh
              veiny tangerine pulp
of buttocks and hip

              the lake floor is so hot
the leaves on the painted eucalyptus
              sparkle

Hunger remembered stories
              how the sun
slanted to deceive the moon
              why mosquitoes whimper
he painted as if light
              blazed from above
to glaze the olive shallows
              and daub
each petal and stalk
              with a live sheen

A woman
              perches
in the bow of a *pirogue*
              tucked in near fronds
her torso's a starred almond
              her gaze
drawn by perspective
              to the azure
center
              where a skiff
glides on its own shadow

The traveler's reflection
        curves
sprigs refract
        from the crescent hull
bound for a smudge
        beyond the far shore

The third figure
        bends
into the weeds
        she's found something
smoked meat or *bukari* perhaps
        he's left behind

           Too late
the boat's already
        inches out of earshot
the long shaft of the oar
        descends
from sky across stick neck
        and knees
straight into coarse water
        a slash
in Hunger's dream

        through it
I stare
        at the lake floor
           and the flames

Letter with Photograph

from: Roger Casement, British Consul to the Belgian Congo
to: E. D. Morel, founder, Congo Free Society; author, *Red
     Rubber*. Liverpool: Congo Free Society Press, 1904.

     May 3, 1903, Leopoldville

My dear Morel,

I want to tell you everything I saw
and what the urge to see which brought us here
has done. A blond-haired mercenary swore
here in my office over drinks
the *Force Publique* massacred Ibiaku.
What shit, I thought, & listened bored
to the cliché adventures journalists dream up—
soup-green jungles, pythons,
leeches, crocodiles *big as big as*...
Africa shrunk to a penny dreadful western—
if you think this innocent you've never cut
the figure English clubs so love—
the witness restored miraculous
from parts unknown,
well-tanned, prone to melancholia
(one sigh and a pillboy will grip his elbow,
thinking atrocities scarred a noble mind).

The squad crept through mud and vines
and got so close, he said, he could hear
the mamas singing and the pestles
pounding manioc—could smell
the palm oil and smoked fish.
They were so close he had to twitch
to fret the tsetse flies that gorged
till stiff as knuckles on his blood
(one slap might warn the villagers).
Finally, at dusk, they started the attack.

Then, before I showed him
the enclosed photograph, he described
and traced in the air
with an ivory letter-opener
certain cicatrices Captain U.V.
instructed the men to carve on female corpses
to make it look like work of a rival tribe.
I glanced up—for the first time wondered *truth*?
He rolled his cuff to show the bites—still fresh.
I followed his malaria-bleared eyes
taking in our British Consulate:
raw teak, framed portrait of the King,
the leaky corrugated tin
that grazes my hair when I stand up.
And all the while his blue pulse
lay there bared for me—to cut
or to detach us—he and I—somehow
from the mutilated bodies pictured here—
the gesture was so natural—
palm up, his forearm hair
the color of the rust stains on this page.

Scald

There is a place in far north Canada
where day breaks the color of tea's
first flush, and if you believe
frost, or just a way
of feeling cold, could grip three
generations then maybe
you've been there, or some such place—
the skin-taut road of your own
spine let's say, smooth as
milk spoons—and even if
you're home, even if home
is Berkeley California where sun's
part of the deal, a chill
wisps over you and the brass
rails, the slo-mo Casablanca
whirring fans of your rave café
blur salmon bright and words
formed and rehearsed on the lush
winding drive up the coast road
freeze in your gorge. In this
Canada, the horizon sharpens. A Canuck
and gaggle of boys issue from a box
house into fierce wind. Work
mills every waking minute;
it is a drudgery I imagine
you can't know—the meals
around you sculpted on pale
china, the service choreographed.
Not that you won't pay. But you
regard the teak, linen, and gold
as if some motif veiled a pistol;
a line blips through your head
like an ad slogan or mantra *life my*
life love my own life. To say this—
you can't yet—but your lover,
the beautiful sleek woman whose voice

has haunted since she phoned,
pregnant, senses it, stays
locked behind the menu's
leather triptych. In the chinky
box house in 1933 a crone
nurses water on a coal
samovar. She is your lover's
grandmother and this, at least,
is hers—this warming of hands before
the day's first task, the day
she accidentally killed her
youngest girl. It's a curse
your lover revealed one lazy
morning months ago, seizing you
from sleep: the scalding
of an infant in the cold
vast waste of Canada. Her curse
then but now, as the waiter
brushes past and the chef
seasons tonight's special
never to have been, you seem
to see the laundry bucket
tense; you feel
close enough to snatch
the child burrowing in the clothes bin
toward sleep, through calico,
toward warmth, forgetfulness.

But when you speak you say *I love
you but I want
nothing to change I want
everything to be just as it was*
and so it is: you're alone, cleaving
blurred redwood cliffs, a bright
wave hissing down through limbs
that shiver like hands feeling
for a child, if you ever risk one.

Letter to Fever

from: Roger Casement
      July 3, 1903 45 miles east of Leopoldville

Brother Fever,

So sick, afraid to write your name and risk
losing dream-sight of the skiff on Lough Erne,
your strong back at the oars, straining
like Caillebotte's floor scrapers—
although you've never been to Ireland
nor seen a modern painting. Brother Fever,
I dream of rubbing your gold back with alcohol
as if distance were varnish I could knead,
belladonna for your eyes, myrrh for love.
Memory must be feeling,
as your namesake Saint Augustine writes,
for yesterday when I heard reports
that one survivor of a massacre
waited across the river, I remembered
a bruise on your smooth thigh, violet
as a love mark or the sky over Lough Erne,
though I've never seen your perfect body hurt.
But when I peered across, no one was there.
Fever felt an absence, refusal
to be witnessed, as if it had been you
who bent at dawn to cup the river water,
then turned your back on tent and dying fire,
brushing back the whippy branches,
toward pain where fever can't be brother.
Agostinho, malaria veils your face,
but peels away at the same time the doubt
that what I most fear, I most yearn for.

The Cornice of the Skull

"Are you too dead?"—"How in the world above
My body fares," he answered,
"I do not know." Such power
Has Ptolomea, that sometimes the soul
Drops hither before death.

Inferno, Canto XXXIII

To lurch, crooning, in moonlight from the pub,
      and wander the Connemara beach,
and grope my tent and collapse, snoring until
      I wake at high tide in the ocean;

to have my car catch fire on the freeway,
      rush begging cups of water, to suffer
the fireman's smirk as he hands me the crisped oil cap
      left unscrewed on the engine block;

to freeze and raise my arms, then sprint into
      deep elephant grass, my skin tingling,
waiting for the bullet from the wild-
      eyed teenage Congolese soldier;

these are the scenes I relive, hope to dream,
      dying, and perhaps just after death,
waving my arms in laughter, saying *yes,*
      from the first I have known this—

or gripping my smashed leg in agony;
      or rocking to music or to loss;
or walking alone, feeling a bird vault
      in my chest or a stone sink—

how I have practiced, stepping through the dream
      awake, the way children imagine
what they most fear, knowing that what
      they imagine best will never be.

How many times have I let my body slip
        out of itself, in dream, the way
my father did? Three times he tried to live
        the dream right to the end—

the first—he almost had it right—just as
        he'd pictured: handing his keys,
his wallet back, waving goodbye, going down
        only to wake, and find himself

still here—but the world dimmed, slivering
        down to a cataracted moon,
and night filling him up until there was
        only a flicker left to die in.

What if no sea or fire consumes, no brain-
        gray bullet flashes once, at last
to blaze the shape I am—a billion instants
        locked in a nerve-comb?

What if I missed it? And the fields and pond
        and sky outside my window go on
darkening, and words still stiffen even
        as they're fingertipped,

and in my skull, where I drown, or writhe in flames,
        or tense as the blood spurts, a voice
drones on, "I thought you lived, still walked the earth,"
        and I reply forever, "But I do."

Letter with Photograph

from: the Reverend W. Holmen Bentley, *Chevalier de l'order Royal du Lion*
to: Roger Casement, Leopoldville

April 2, 1903 Mission Kibongo, Ibiaku

Dear Sir Roger:

I thank you for the tar, but rain—
if three month's pitiless sheets can be called rain—
has rotted thatch beyond repair:
we'll need tin if ever we're to sleep.
Friend, my gums bleed.
I burn and freeze, flies sting,
and I've gone hours, whole days at a time
into that place where pain brims
and I lie just numb. It's enough
to make me wish with the old gnostics:
let there be no body,
just eyes and lush green vegetable soul.
Let eyes flourish. Forest and sky.
Sight so keen that when a bird darts
I don't track flight but watch
the shape that was flash up
and crumple in bright air. It's fever—
both worlds in me shivering.
But in these photographs, which no doubt
you've studied before reading this dispatch—
which world? I see you, friend,
the way I see those birds, the way
I still envision a field of hacked flesh.
Smoke led me there but what made me
take photographs—then nurse them
visible in the chinked dark of my hut—
is thinking I'd die inside not knowing
(and you, here twenty years to my three months,
must know) if it's in them—

the ones we've come to save—or in the air—
this contagion that makes men kill
and cut Christ's cross in flesh.

And so I send this with the Roi de Belge
and Korzeniowski—himself
a well man last month
when he unloaded tar but now,
returning from further up the river,
so sick that if by miracle he survives
and you receive from him my question,
you'll have touched, as I felt touching his,
God's trembling hand.

In Pére Paul's Room

Mission Kibongo, Ibiaku

A woman stripped
        here in this room
                you start
again the tale
        your hands
                lock in your lap
your stiff back rocks
        forward on starched sheets
                her wail
rings here from thirty years ago
        the bed springs squeak
                the jags of wallpaper
have heard this so many times
        they blur
                to smoke of rag torches
teak masks & raffia skirts
        close in
                on the tin tray
        the fruit basket
                lights up with
curiosity & smoke
        so fierce
                you blink &
stutter once
        again
                she stripped
to the waist
        it was a funeral here
                thirty years ago
you came to this lake to sanctify
                a heathen ceremony
father of light—father who gives bread
        you piped
                your memorized Swahili text

while drums beat & torches closed on
           your fear so intense
                     you felt naked
underneath your stiff
           brocaded chasuble
                     you did not understand
her wail
           that pierces
                     thirty years
something to do with *light*
           you don't know
                     what miracle or sin
reveals her now—
           her breasts
                     flapping against her—
           the paps
heavy as mud on a spade tip
           I watch
                     your palms stick
to the glass of syrupy wine
           the mangoes
                     light up
photographs of relatives long dead
           watch you
                     rock forward
steady your palsied fingers
           as she stumbles
                     near, you
try to pierce
           with a tin knife
                     the skin
of an iodine-soaked pulp &
           she wails
                     a tongue you did not
understand
           as the blade hops
                     & I take

the papaya from your hands & slice
            daydreaming breasts
                        sunned for me
in my own country
            sweet taste
                        of California wine
& belly lint &
            fur, undoing
                        a lace bra—or
breasts glimpsed on a beach
            or slicking nude
                        through blue smoke
to the tick tick tick of film strips while

            gently, you release
the neck
            of the tottering
                        carafe, your hands
appeal to me as if I saw
            her slink smoke-dark into the room
                        I turn
& crack a rib of the venetian blind
            outside
                        the tended jacarandas
flame, *light up* she must have cried
            meaning enlighten
                        you insist
I squint at fierce light glinting off the lake & now
            you rise, you
                        shuffle toward me
sure she tears a flowered blouse out of the wallpaper
            for you, for
                        you alone, your one
convert in this blinding sun to wine,
            beads, chasuble
                        light, her ghost voice

rises in your throat, your fingers reach
toward me to take a halved
papaya
as if across real distances

Letter to Photograph

from: E.D. Morel
      July 9, 1903, Liverpool

Casement,

Although we've never met I feel I know you.
Not as everyone who hears your exploits does—
not as the incarnation of vague yearnings.
Even our taciturn Korzeniowski
spin yarns about you sauntering
through unspeakable wilderness with nothing
but a native porter and two brindled dogs,
to emerge months later, he says—
gaunt, grimed—but flourishing your blackthorn
as if just back from a stroll through Phoenix Park.
the Congolese call you *Monafuma*—"Noble's Son"
but also "Boy's Rod," Koreniowski said,
and slid this photograph across my desk:
A tall, spare, English gent reclining
in a rattan chair. Yes, I know you.
I've never been south of Liverpool but still
I recognize the kind that manages
to keep his trousers pressed in Africa.
Years before your gents cut checks
to my crusade against the tyrant
I rose to the rank of dock clerk by my fists.
Dim light, but I didn't flee to Africa,
I taught myself Engels and watched
my brothers live like beasts. Finally I understood
the cyphers I logged each day—
Winchesters shipped out,
ivory and rubber shipped back in—
meant bugger the adventure—
everywhere was just the same as here.
And knowing, do you think I stare
into the limpid eyes beneath your

country gentleman's slouch brim
with admiration? It is my manuscript,
not Conrad's fancy that will fix you
in time's frame. *Red Rubber*
is pure fact: I assure you
of the utmost accuracy to the last
detail: even the rubber trees
that illustrate each chapter
were traced from horticultural manuals;
the India ink Goliath Beetle
planned for the frontispiece was drawn
faithfully to scale by my own hand.

Mazembé

Across a decade and lost distances
I remember Lubumbashi and the night
we played *Mazembé* on a blacktop
under a full moon. Sharp shadows
and the warp of the dead basketball,
they're with me here in timelessness
where mind and heart knit silently.
Mazembé: Swahili for "Bulldozer,"
the class of the Katanga circuit,
four six-foot hulks forged in *Gécamines*,
plus *Vedette*, the star, head waiter
at the Greek Club with a gold tooth
and a manic will to drive no way but right.

We were three Peace Corps brats,
a diamond smuggler and the cultural attaché,
rumored a spy. But to *les fanatiques*,
a swaying, three-deep out-of-bounds line,
we were *Les Americains—Les*
because the only ones they'd seen,
and despite our cons and gaudy tank-tops
some doubted we were real
since but for me, we looked *Zairois*:

Reggie, a slick 6'2" Duke guard;
Big Clarence, the Georgia linebacker;
Turbo, with great wheels and a schizo passport;
Sir Godfrey—*le vieux* at forty—
first black player ever in the SEC—
once he was jackknifed by a redneck fan
and he showed us the new moon scar on his smooth paunch;
and me: 6'3" 160 after lunch,
with a high school jump shot that lured
Jimmy V to weaken my knees with hope
of stardom, a new father,
and 800 bucks from Bucknell U.
His phone call peaked my American career.

In Lubumbashi I was real to the touch,
not merely to these lines that echo
across a decade and lost distances.

I was in love and twice I lay
awake all night with happiness.

And though the next ten years locked her and me
in tiny rooms that buzz now in my skull,
those first nights promised sleep
and the long full rainbow pattern of a life.

Mazembé trained on blacktop barefoot
chanting *Mazembé bomaye!*
They trounced the pride of college kids I coached
(I learned French in huddles—"pick" was *pique*;
"shoot" was *shooté* with a hand flip) until finally
I put myself in, missed three prayers
and went red when *msungu est paresseux*
was translated—"the white guy's lazy."
Crazed for revenge I got myself traded
for two pairs of tire-retread sneakers
and a new Dr. J ABA ball.
But even the ivory the Belgian priest
who bought me smuggled to build a gym
and skim the best toughs off the L'shi streets
wasn't enough to beat *Mazembé*.
They snapped the full-court press I chalked my thugs through,
turning the game into a lay-up drill.

And so *the Americans* was my own idea.

In Lubumbashi American meant TESL
and Sunday Rob Roy's at the Consulate.
It meant big red bikes and baseball caps and beads.
But being in love, I loved the thing I was.
Each caricature seemed laughable and precious—

I loved our *franglais* and our ambling
with bulging backpacks through the *marché*.
I paced before my frosh declaiming:
"I celebrate MYSELF, and sing MYSELF"
flinging my hands worldward as they smirked
as murmured in mock-trance *Whit-man Whit-man*.
The days fit snug to nights, amazing now,
drifting in shades, undulating shapes:
smoke coils, lanteen panels,
and each flame shadow tingling to the touch.

That night under strange stars and swelling moon
we high-fived, juked, and showboated our warm-ups.
It had been hard getting the guys up:
I'd dogged Clarence, and bribed Reggie
from his bush post two days off
with a night life that earned this town
the name "Evil Elizabethville."
Godfrey was skittish being seen with Turbo,
and Turbo was nervous being seen. But though
we'd never even seen each other play,
we fanned to the opening circle like one hand opening.
The pleasure was talking trash, was being
on this tar rectangle in Africa at home.
The pleasure was sadness we were only five
who'd been an entire world. And she was there.

These dreamt lines dream her as she was that night:
small ringless hands, bright nimbus of dark hair,
her aura of grace and mockery as she reached,
bent slightly from a spiritual waist
to snatch the towel I flung.
These nightmares, bright as ointment,
flay me to viscera and unsheathed nerve:
any of a billion clock ticks—
each an incarnation—splinters to life:
licking her arched foot after a bee sting;

sliding naked down a summer slope;
tonight it is the towel's frayed wings
opening toward her hands, her hands opening
a chasm: the still night, *Vedette*,
Mazembé, and the close-packed crowd.

Reggie sparked first; he blurred
past midcourt pressure, froze, then
performed a feat never before witnessed:
he dribbled through his legs and dished to Clarence
slicing in. The crowd gaped,
a high voice keened *rej-jie*,
and we five heard electric hoards
chanting REG-GIE to the Bronx sky.

But this was Katanga, forbidden name,
echoing recent slaughter. Katanga,
where Tshombé was uncrowned king,
where Lumumba, half-dead, groveling,
was made to eat his constitution.
Katanga, where rebels with fetishes
strong enough to bend Mobutu's rifles
swept out of the bush to take Kolwesi;
where government troops shot whites before fleeing,
to force the U.N. mercenaries to fight.
These were the rumors murmured over drinks
at the Macreese, Karavia, the Park,
the velvet, malachite-glitzed lounges
where ex-pats, wrung to wraiths, hung on.
But this night, we were myth—
Rej-jie was *fetisheur*; the rock flowed
silver between charmed forms:
our charged, accomplishment bodies—
jump shot, slash and drive;
even before my second wind
we pulled out to a 10-2 lead.

Anger and joy came easily those days,
particles knotting, bursting, but that night
for the first time I saw rage contained.
Vedette spun baseline right, head faked,
and gut-elbowed Big Clarence. He gagged,
doubled, then spluttered at the ref,
"*il a presque moi TUE!*" No call.
I had to waltz Godfrey off when the star flashed
the same grin he served with *cappuccino*
and I saw then what *Mazembé* wanted from this game.
They ran straight lanes, give-and-go's,
and a funky weave cribbed out of Naismith's guide.
Their antique set shots looked like trophies spasming
but they clawed each board, and sniffed our shorts on D;
and at the half, the score was tied.

Jack Sullivan, crew-cut maniac
coach of Fordham Prep, once slapped
me at half-time for saying "Fuck."
I should have walked, or smacked him,
but I sat, red-faced, feeling the sting
numb my cheek and will until
it seemed I peered at lockers
and shifting eyes of eleven boys,
till then my team, from a great distance.
Sometimes when I am reached into and grabbed
I am that boy. Jack loved us—
so he said—for this we called him *bent*
and snickered when he bawled after each loss.
To wring love out of flesh,
reach in with hands or words—just try.
That's how it was the night I breathe hard
Now to keep from entering—
from swallowing me—the night
last month she peered through me in moonlight,
"Too far, too gone for love."

"Positive Imaging," whispers
the owl-faced senior therapist,
zinging my head with Prozac, sedatives.
"Write pictures of the good; the mind
is a made place, can be re-made."

And so I float towards Africa,
full moon, and the dense, swaying crowd.
Starting the second half I felt the touch:
Reggie sensed it, fed me
in the corner, elbow, post.
I was unconscious, zoned, untouchable—
as when, a boy, alone in winter parks,
I'd shoot till my paws bled—it was the cure
for being me—I was West, Havlicek—
not a scarlet lightbulb pulsing against a slap.

The touch—the hoop was a glazed wafer
and my body, slight as a bow,
chin tilted, elbow cocked,
flickered in night air. The touch—
echoed in words, and words only an omen
for the way the self, supple as a tongue,
speaks and is heard. Lovers,
we felt it, ached after it, fading.
Touch: to glide and turn fishlike
in the world, inside
the other—a new being, translucent
rose globe unbound by skin.

It doesn't last, even a night.
The hands grope, the mind shrinks
to a pea in fog, until in
moonlight last month when she reached
into me finally I was not there
or anywhere.

The rest of the game's a dream
of struggling through swaths
of cotton—*Mazembé* swarming, our limbs
gone spidery. We kept it close
on instinct and cheap fouls,
hobbling on blisters, sucking wind.
I dogged *Vedette*—this man who flamed
into himself and into us
between flaked lines, then
vanished in a maze
of gestures, smiles, and nods.

From a place that once was and now is
merely cadence echoed in a nowhere
the shrinks call clinical depression,
but which Catullus knew as
"a paralysis which creeps from limb to limb,
driving all former laughter from the heart,"
an eerie place Bird found,
suddenly half out of his magnificent self
while pain seared the branches of his back,
I cling to the night against *Mazembé*
even in the not-now nowhere.
I recall the ease, the sweet
exhaustion and the beer, strangers
pumping my hand, the scorekeeper
waving crinkled loose-leaf proof
that this night did take place. "Ah,
Mazembé yes, too much," he sighed.
"But tonight, *Philippe*,
tonight you were with us."

Letter to Ireland

from: Roger Casement
to: Agnes Newman

July 12, 1903, Ibiaku

My dear sister,

So you think your man John Redmond
will redeem the Chief?
But Parnell lives his dream beyond his end—
he is more real as shadowy Dead King
than when he muddled speeches in Mayo.
Alive, how out of place he seemed—
stone-faced ascendancy do-gooder
stilting clichés from such height
he drove rain into the upturned faces
of his bovine worshippers. Remember him
saying Kettle's name would be a household word?
But I've chewed Ireland's cud long enough
among the flies of Leopoldville—
Sir Roger Casement, His Majesty's Vice-Consul—
presiding as the pageantry of suffering
awes new upturned faces.
And so I pocketed your letter,
trudged east a hundred miles to answer here.
Lost in the sun's glare, I dreamed
I'd sip palm wine by this sourceless river,
write from deep in some nameless well of blood.
But here turns out to be somewhere made up—
some place I wanted to call Eden—
where the ice emerald that scorched my soul at birth
with penal laws, famine, orange drums
would refract into the infinite
hues of palm wine, leaf, and sky.

Here, yesterday, a man
feathered like a bird wept in my arms.

He was rank with blood and palm oil
and I confess the bile missionaries take
for righteousness rose in my throat.
Then I heard, between his sobs,
my name—last heard 20 years ago—
Monafuma—and I knew this place
I wanted to be nowhere was Ibiaku,
where once a chief placed meat on the quivering tongue
of the young adventurer I was—
first white man he had ever seen—
saying take, *Monafuma*. And I knew
the rumors of a massacre were true.

Nina, you must think I don't remember—
being a small boy—spitting
at the frosted oaks where papist waifs barbed shrikes—
how we unhooked and buried with all righteous hate
their bloody offense to the pure air
of Ulster's winter. Yesterday
as my chief's son scorched my mind
with images of devastation I saw
the arch of that spit flame
to a torched beehive launched by my own kin
in a barrage of fire—and it burst
upon me for the first time who I was—
as if before I hadn't known even
why I speak English or what love feels like.
Nina, Rory I am, here *Monafuma*—
brother to these also dispossessed.

from *Phantom Signs*

The Book I Almost Wrote

I almost wrote a book. I wrote almost all of a book. Nearly every word. I reached the end. I edited and revised. I wrote the book many ways. I wrote it many times. I wrote it in prose and verse. I studied it. I learned almost all of it by heart. I didn't write the blurbs or flap copy; you're not supposed to write them, or if you do, you pretend to be someone else. I didn't decide the ISBN or PCIP or list price. I did not design the cover or delineate the gutters or select the font. I did not choose my name. But of the words conventionally ascribed to the author, I wrote almost every one.

It was a book about a paradox.

    A. Writing a book is hard.

    B. It's supposed to look easy.

As Yeats says, "A line will take us hours maybe / But if it does not seem a moment's thought / Our stitching and unstitching have been nought."

My book took a long time. It began as another book altogether. "To Banquet with the Worthy Ethiopians: A Memoir of Life Before the Alphabet" was the working title.

A memoir is especially hard unless you are famous, in which case you get someone else to write it for you, or at least edit. The other problem is that people hate being flattened from three dimensions to two, so there can be issues when you write about living people. They can write back.

Not being famous, I had to write alone. And the people I made two-dimensional were dead or their faces were masked. The memoir was set in a Long Island Police Athletic League boys' camp. In the summer of seventh grade—which the memoir calls the summer of Item 265—I spent my first nights away from home. The summer was bad. Horrible. Not just the gruel and bugs and sweaty shorts and sandy bunks and endless games of war ball. Adolescent boys are cruel to anyone different, and I was different. As the book says,

> My body grilled in Rouse-like sentences,
> Elongating while resisting girth
> Until the chest caved in and the fingers of one hand
> Could encircle a thigh. The ears unhinged.
> The cartilaginous right speared like an antler.

The left lobe drooped below the jaw.
Eyelids pinked. Lashes crusted.
The trunk roiled, mapping new pustules.
Bloody pus clotted morning sheets.

These aren't the words I wrote in the memoir. I've lost those words completely. This is a later verse interpolation. But in every version the boys were hideous, and at the time it seemed that this was the only world I would ever inhabit: a nightmare landscape of terror and humiliation. The hoodlums promised that on the last night of camp they would all piss into a bucket and sneak into my bunk and pour the bucket over me. I ran to the camp office and made a collect call to my parents and begged them to come get me. They came. None of this is in any of the versions of the book I almost wrote, because I wanted to avoid dealing directly with those who were still extant. Instead, I focused on the Trojan War, and W. H. D. Rouse's prose translation of the *Iliad*. Thus the Rouse-like sentences.

For this paradoxical state of affairs (A & B) I blame Homer. Before he started to "articulate sweet sounds together" on the page, bards rocked and chanted, feeding the voice, and the voice fed the utterance. Or that's the way I had it in my book. But I wrote the book crouched over a screen with my eyes watering and sudden beeps from Facebook and my right foot going numb, and everything had to be constructed and verified and revised down to the nub.

Besides Homer, there were two other obstacles.

A. I had become a publisher. On the kind of whim that made Mickey Rooney launch movie musicals, I had started, with two cronies, a literary press. Etruscan, we called it, a little dizzy with self-delight. We schemed to use money from Stags, my rich friend, to hire labor while Mooney, my novelist friend, and I would select the books and meet writers and lunch at the Algonquin.

Then 9/11 happened. Bill Heyen, eminent poet and towering anthologist, proposed a book called "September 11, 2001: American Writers Respond." He wanted to capture America's first reaction to the tragedy. But Etruscan didn't, so to speak, exist. We had no distributor or designer or marketers or deal-cutters or editors. We knew about publishing the way foodies know about restaurants: we knew what we liked. But we did have Stags's money. So we hired a bright-looking lad and rented an office in Chestertown, MD. I was on sabbatical in Providence and had fallen head over heels for a woman 20 years younger and I saw everything as if through a sparkling veil and 9/11 didn't seem real. So we told Bill OK and he buttonholed 127 writers including John Updike and Erica Jong and Lucille Clifton and Robert Pinsky and he even made up a few writers like Edwina Seaver and Rose Carmine Smith with a wink to Joyce Carol Oates.

Then we contacted a pro named Tom Woll who had made his bones at Vanguard with Dr. Seuss back in the days of three martini lunches, and I met Tom halfway between Yonkers and Providence at a bagel shop on Rte 17 and Tom hooked us up with Mortimer Mint, a Dickensian refugee who made his fortune distributing the *Guinness Book of World Records*, and Morty sold ten thousand copies and we thought publishing was a cinch and then 8,500 copies came back— we didn't know about returns—and Stags coughed up more money and bailed us out.

By now I was a full-time publisher and people sent me manuscripts by the hundreds and we had to fire the bright-looking kid for fraud and I drove to the foot of the Chesapeake Bay Bridge and rendezvoused with our new managing editor at Hemingway's and handed over two armloads of files. Suddenly I was immersed in something I had always avoided: business. Now I could confab with my college pals about cost benefit and cash flow, and I learned that you can't treat employees like students because if students fail, so what? And manuscripts kept coming and I lost a few friends and some sleep and many of the poems were good, but not that good, or all good in the same way: a setting and observation about the setting developing into three or four related observations strung together in a short time span; usually walking was involved, sometimes driving. All were rectangular and they began to look like clumsy interpolations translated from Etruscan and it was mile after loose-stepped mile of chopped prose. Did I say all? Not so. Some were served straight from academic Delphi, where the oracle was deconstructed into semiotic salads only a tower-dweller could digest.

Poems are so enigmatic. Each emerges from some private darkness which publication does not entirely dispel. They are composed of such a paucity of words. We choose to trust their silences. But we approach with caution. No one wants to be taken in by a false poem. An accidental verse. So we screen them the way we screen blind dates. We hear from teachers or colleagues, reviewers and enthusiasts. We peruse the book: the colophon, the pedigree, the blurbs that confirm value with words like "luminous" and "sublime," the mysterious or catchy titles: *Return to a Room Lit by a Glass of Milk*, *Preface to a Twenty-Volume Suicide Note*, *Autonecrophilia*, *The Book of Orgasms*, or *What Narcissism Means to Me*. By the time we open the book and scan the creamy page with its noble Garamond, we are prepared to give each poem what William Stafford called "a certain kind of attention."

These conditions do not prevail in the publisher's office. Publishers receive only a brief cover and we must address the draft of the internationally unknown poet without the benefit of context. No private darkness, no magic, and certainly no rarity. There are thousands. They have no reticence. They come, as Philip Dacey says, "so encumbered."

Reading unsolicited manuscripts mars publishers. Print is limitless. If you are not a publisher, you may have no idea of how many serviceable poems are making their doleful rounds. At conferences or bars or beaches or subway platforms, we publishers pass one another and nod in silence, recognizing the vampiric gaze and slow shamble of the endless scroll.

Whatever their quality and number, these submissions were complete, and so they were better than what I was doing at my other desk, trying to write a memoir. Albert Lord who studied bards in Yugoslavia said that when oral poets learned to write, they lost the ability to compose spontaneously, and I thought that maybe something analogous had occurred and that after becoming a publisher I'd never be able to compose poetry again. And so I scribbled sentence after sentence until I was walled in, and the memoir was on the other side of the wall.

B. I have a love-hate relationship with sentences. I love the freedom and the buoyancy and the way they go on and on, executing a flip turn at the margin. But, they do go on. I compose them only in daylight or lamplight, always alone. They can't be learned by heart; they can't breathe for long away from print. They are—or at least my sentences seem—foreign. Sentences have no darkness. They are devoid of mystery. If you think of something that might go in a sentence, you stick it in. Bent on transposing whole cartons of toxic reality onto the page, you get woozy. Like I say, it's a paradox. So one day I went swimming.

I have a love-hate relationship with swimming. I love the freedom and buoyancy, the reach and kick. I love the glimpse of light when I suck in air, and the black lane lines refracting on exhale. I love the flip turn, and the full-stretch glide two beats long. At the finale, I speed crawl to the deep end and jackknife down to trace the tile insignia, staying as long as my lungs last, letting the rising take me, effortless. But a swimming pool is the place where I feel most alone, trapped in my mind. There's no end, no arc. Swimming doesn't correspond to anything I do anywhere else. Water is, finally, a foreign element which I cannot inhabit.

That October afternoon in 2010 I slipped into the chlorine water and began my regimen. But I got through only four laps when I felt pressure in my chest, and my breath went shallow. Later that day I was wheeled into St. Elizabeth's for coronary triple bypass surgery.

After a week in the hospital, I spent three months in my rocking chair by the fire, in the living room of our ramshackle cottage looking south on a park in Youngstown, Ohio, where I've lived for thirty years. Three decades, three months, three hours of unconsciousness. What matter? Youngstown is not home. That dreamscape has another name. I call it Queens. It's no Ithaca, my Queens—in fact it now doppelgangs Seoul and Baghdad, as once, in Father's voice, it was called Galway. Any destination, given time and distance, eludes naming.

At home in my rocking chair in the fall of 2010, I clutched the teddy bear with the cracked heart bib the nurses give heart patients to keep us from tearing the incision. I read, I binged on Netflix, I napped. Many patients, a pamphlet told me, feel depression when they return from heart surgery. But I felt peace. It helped that my wife was home and friends drove hundreds of miles to visit; it helped that I had colleagues to take over my courses and a managing editor to handle business at Etruscan; it helped that the autumn passed almost imperceptibly through the bay window facing the park. Life is good, I thought. And still think.

Then I turned to the pages that had been the memoir. How distant—a world glimpsed through fogged goggles. What matter what actually happened one summer fifty years ago? What matter, this breaking and remaking—wading through sentences that could never be heard at night or out on a walk; sentences that always needed light, and were always read alone?

And then, rubbing my bear's fur in my rocking chair in the autumn of 2010 deep in midlife, I began to rock. Back and forth, just as I had long ago in Queens in front of the hi-fi, rocking on hands and knees while Father's Clancy Brothers albums scratched unearthly tunes about a home so far off it might have been Ethiopia. Backward to the sea I rocked, forward into a world of goddesses and fiends.

As I rocked and chanted in Youngstown after surgery and dove deep to the bottom of memory-tracing runes, I began to see that there was no home, no element anyone could own or even belong to, except for a moment reaching for a single line. The reach is home, or hospital bed; and the line is the insignia of yearning. Scanning sentences, I knew that I didn't want to write a memoir to remake a vanished world. I didn't want my breath to go shallow. I didn't want to feel the way I had felt all those years ago with Rouse: knowing something lay beneath, some rhythmic present tense that sentences could only describe or obscure.

So I began my own translation: from sentences to lines. I started transposing history, as Timothy Findley says, "into another key, which is mythology." Backward toward Queens, forward into the Police Camp, I began to translate my sentences into blank verse—remaking or breaking or making up a life from a great distance— the distance of having been, briefly, dead.

From a page-bound home I rocked to a place where

> A child composes the rooftree of a house.
> Verse tunes his breath—iamb
> Of upturned face, caesura of sinews,
> The ache of denouement pricked by a 'huh'
> That triggers the next line. And within,

Angle of toe and knuckle, cant of head,
Each phrase devising its own signature.

In the belly of a house the child soars
Over the mountains and the wine-dark sea.

Every plunge backward meets the thud
Of flesh on bone, spurring the thrust forward.

Writing is hard. It's supposed to look easy. But there's a third leg to the paradox: writing isn't even supposed to look like writing. It's supposed to seem like utterance. It's supposed to be heard, or overheard. It's supposed to appear as if it's from somewhere else. This is where the book I almost wrote was headed. It was about life before the alphabet, not just childhood, but the eons of myth-time before Homer started to write things down. A time when "eternity brightened the rim of each instant." Without the alphabet to keep time straight, everything could slide from now to forever and back in a generation or an instant. There was no breach between everything that happened and all that did not. Of course, it's another paradox to write a book about the futility of writing a book, though in many ways all books are about that. Sometimes I think that the last three thousand years of poetry compose a long elegiac wail for a time when "lines were conceived and spoken in one breath." And anyway, I didn't write a book about it. I wrote most of a book.

Years went by, and Etruscan grew and flourished and people kept sending me manuscripts and a few of them I published. Every month I finished a verse chapter. At the beginning of each month I almost drowned, overwhelmed by all I hadn't written, and by the end of each month I flew through the house. Over and over it happened, the drowning and flying, the rocking and chanting, till finally I was done. And because I had spent a decade reading manuscripts, I knew that this was different. It wasn't sentences. It wasn't chopped prose. I even changed the name. I called it, "To Banquet with the Ethiopians: A Memoir of Life Before the Alphabet." Nearly the same, but different.

I found Broadstone Books and Larry Moore introduced me to Buffalo Trace and the Kentucky Derby and he brought in a genius designer, Laurie Powers, to dress the words beautifully and we all edited and extrapolated and amplified and nitpicked and scoured the net for images and fonts. And one day a UPS box arrived at my house across from the park in Ohio. I tore open the carton and scattered the peanuts and inhaled the new book smell and caressed the gloss. My book. The book I wrote. I thought I'd written all of it. The whole thing. But I hadn't.

That night I read the words that had taken all those years and had finally broken through the wall of sentences. I read almost to the end, and it was strange because in this beautiful codex the words seemed as if they came from somewhere else and I didn't remember writing any of them.

Until I came to the second-to-last page. That's when I found out I had not written all the book. I wrote most of it. Almost all. But on the second-to-last-page, in the last stanza, I read a line I definitely knew I had not composed. A line I had never seen.

It was "Fearless fleeing naked toward Roba."

I knew Fearless. I knew he fled. But Fearless was running out of time into the sea. He was running out of his body; he was swimming, he was almost drowning. Where was this unknown place, Roba?

It's a paradox to write a book about the way the alphabet walls us into our separate lives; it's strange to work so hard to make simple utterance.

In the beginning of the book the scrivener admits that his Homeric stand-in, Thersites, might just be an inkblot. Writing is hard. It's not trustworthy. It has the taste of death. And now it ended in a place I did not know.

I called Laurie and she sent me back a scanned page of the galleys which I had scrawled over and drawn arrows in. And in the margin, among the glyphs and arabesques, there it was.

"Fearless fleeing naked toward Roba."

Reading it now, as a late interpolator, I think the scrivener meant to say not Roba but "the sea" and he didn't mean the line to be there anyway, but somewhere else. But there it was.

That night I walked through the house feeling lost and overwhelmed as at the beginning of each month and it was even worse since I was a publisher and had dealt with all classes of screw-ups and had invented protocols and procedures and here was my book from another publisher and it was lost in some place I'd never heard of.

Then Laurie sent me a google map. A map to this place that was invented out of a misread hand. A map showing that Roba is not nowhere. It is a water-way in Ethiopia, where Fearless was always trying to flee to escape the world, and time, and the boys at summer camp whom the memoir never names.

And that meant that the voice that Homer had heard and then silenced when he learned the alphabet and became a publisher, was still whispering, here, in this imperfect text.

Yes. Homer knew those waters. He had tried to swim out of his skin to Roba, Ethiopia. But who knows Homer? In the goodly company of the dead, he sways on a far shore. Truth? History? He is immersed in his own rocking and chanting. He is christened No One. His home, one ancient scroll declares, is called Ithaca. And Telemachus is his father.

It could be Homer was composed only of utterance and he made up his own father. It could be he never had a body. And what if he did? I know now that the body, like the alphabet, is a foreign element, composed of countless microbial beings swimming forever in the dark until the sternum is cleaved and the fugitives are brought to ghastly light.

Between what is called me and what is not, a child still rocks, composing the rooftree of a house. He reaches for Roba, like another element. He sings—I sing—as if this element were home, if only for a heartbeat.

from *To Banquet with the Ethiopians:*
A Memoir of Life Before the Alphabet

Book I   Between Moon and Cup

> Let people laugh at my prematurely gray hair.
> My answer is a wine cup, full
> Of the moon, drowned in the river.
>
> —Su Tung P'o

On a shelf between the moon and my wine cup
Folded in the catalog of ships
I keep a secret list. Inventory
Of everything that happens and does not.
At night in my silent office I reach up
And push aside the artificial plant,
And tip Fagles' *Iliad* from its niche.
I inscribe, erase, and rearrange.
Then I rock, chanting to moon and cup.

Item 265 is a wine-dark slash—
Ur-script—a cave figure or totem.
When tilted to the moon the form resolves
Into a child. Then a burning city.
Finally a word—a strange name:
As best as I make out it reads *Thersites*.

If this necromantic glyph welting my list
Conjures a crippled fool from Homer,
Then drowned is the moon shimmering in my cup,
And my heart plying its verse through storms of blood,
And the uneasy peace that comes from chanting lists.

Before the alphabet locked his name in time,
Did Homer rock, chanting to moon and cup?
Is it to remember or forget?
Since verse has been sentenced to be read,
Hexameters could wash up on a beach
Anywhere in the last 3000 years,
Say, with a clubhouse and a horseshoe of pine cabins
Like my New York Police Athletic Camp
Of the distant summer of Item 265.

Like Thersites I'd been sent to become a man,
Though unsteady on my adolescent pins.

The heroes of Thersites' beach camp
Were Agamemnon, Achilles, and Odysseus.
And so were the heroes of my beach camp.
I named them from the paperback I'd nicked
From a bin outside the Main Street 5&10.
"A Great Adventure Story," it was billed.
"The Greatest War Novel Ever Penned."
Perched on a spavined bunk I clutched the book
And when Achilles or Odysseus
Or royal Agamemnon strode by,
I buried my nose till pages came unglued.
"Plain English of the Plain Story of Homer,"
W.H.D. Rouse claimed, but his sentences
Unstrung syntax, dismembering
Parts of speech, spewing eponyms.
It seemed impossible that I would ever grasp

*My lords, and you their subjects, for you I pray that the gods who dwell in Olympos
may grant you to sack Priam's city, and to have a happy return home! but my dear
daughter—set her free, I beseech you, and accept this ransom, and respect Apollo-
Shootafar the son of Zeus.*

Yet somewhere in this mail-fisted word hoard
Sheathed in paragraphs and studded with compounds
Was hidden, it was said, the secret to manhood.

At night in the full moon revising lists
I think that if 265 is a Greek pawn
Bawling against fate it signifies
Only that a child in a distant summer
Failed to master an overstuffed prose pony.
Perhaps I can erase. Or at least downgrade.
But why Thersites? Why not Rouse or Homer?

In the *Iliad* Thersites, a foot-soldier,
Limps into Book II where I crease my list.
Agamemnon has succumbed to Zeus's dream
Urging a dawn attack to shame Achilles.
But the general fears his exhausted troops won't fight,
So he masses the army, curses the rising sun,
And pretends to bend to divine implacable will.
"Never will Argives sack Holy Troy,"
He wails. "We must sail home disgraced."
But his ploy backfires. His veterans
Rush into the surf and shoulder hulls.
Axes hack cables. Oars tumble.
Then Odysseus enters, sees the folly
Of Empty-Helmeted Agamemnon.
He turns the army back and heaps the shame
On Thersites, who's crying to go home—
Just as I was, the summer of 265.

That summer long ago was the summer of love,
The summer cities burned, and the summer
My father's heart drowned chasing a goddess.
Chanted, love and arson flame into verse.
But my body grilled in Rouse-like sentences—
Elongating while resisting girth
Until the chest caved in and the fingers of one hand
Could encircle a thigh. The ears unhinged:
The cartilaginous right speared like an antler,
The left lobe drooped below the jaw.
Eyelids pinked, lashes crusted.
The trunk roiled, mapping new pustules.
Bloody pus spotted morning sheets.

On the morning of Agamemnon's dream of victory
Thersites wakes drenched with sleeplessness.
Nights in camp were always the same:
Toads and spiders and shrieking cicadas.

But now Thersites can't believe his eyes.
The army is splashing in the sea.
It's here he utters the only sentence
In twenty-four books I was sure I understood.
"Let us all sail home," he cries,
"And leave this man to digest his gorge of prizes."

The summer of 265 the prizes were
Plastic figurine trophies and tin badges.
The only fleet, aluminum canoes.
Our fathers were the police so no one dared
Sail home. We were drilled
In war-ball, team-wrestling, and hunt the runt.
The day was regimented combat.
The foe was nattering and skylarking,
Out-of-step and belly-button-gazing.
Even if I couldn't rock to him,
I clung to Rouse like a hostage's passport.

Scriveners say Homeros may mean hostage
Which would explain how every chant got sentenced.
But what if rocking made it possible
To alter course, zigzag between
Plain English and relentless fate,
And sail past the summer of 265?

Imagine for instance that Odysseus
Fails to enter the mayhem on the beach.
Fails to intervene for Agamemnon.
Instead, he rocks. Chants a line. Vanishes.
No one turns the army from the sea.
Legions of epic sentences disbanded.
Empires leveled, narratives destroyed.

Arching past the full of a scrivener's life,
(And scrivener in some dialects means hostage)

With my heart panting from waves of fierce attacks,
I see a host of reasons to disappear:
Empty-helmeted provosts clawing deans
Who backbite petulant junior colleagues through
Ages of betrayals and conspiracies
To the world's first committee when Odysseus,
Called to the Trojan War by Agamemnon,
Feigned madness and was forced to choose between
A life of peace at home and his son's life.
Now by disappearing from Book II,
Odysseus could avenge his ancient shame
And undo every cause to the end of time.

Then he hears Thersites' barbaric yawp.
His eyes fix on the rocking, chanting grunt—
The trunk pressed wrongways by god's thumb,
Unfeigned madness frozen into fate.
Odysseus' heart clenches, his limbs go numb.

In the days of his feigned madness, Odysseus
Had slathered his chest with gore, lowed like a bull,
Zigzagged a rusty plough through beach and weeds.
Though it started as a ploy to dodge the draft,
He'd loved being mad: shifting shape
From bird to beast, lightning to pellucid moon.
Simply by rocking on hands and knees
He was everywhere at once and nowhere.
Backward to the sea, forward he rocked
Into a world of goddesses and fiends.

On the beach of 265 Rouse's heroes
Crowded too close for me to rock or chant
Though alone under the moon I might hum.
I didn't believe becoming a man would help.
I didn't know my heart would ever drown.
I would never escape my warping bag of skin.

On Homer's beach, Odysseus can't escape
The sentences of the catalog of ships.
But before he rallies the army and saves the day,
He stands a moment mesmerized
By a figure that he cannot grasp.
It might be Thersites. It might be
A picture of a child in a burning city.
It might be his own goddess-lorn heart,
Drowning. "No one," the hero cries,
Raising his scepter to strike his nemesis,
"No one alive more bent with shame than you."
As the club falls, Time commences,
My list swells, and Odysseus becomes
Finally a soldier of Agamemnon.

Between moon and cup can I now disappear?
For all that my heart rocks in a blood-storm
I'm frozen in one sentence, "Sail home."
And Homer is held hostage inside Rouse,
And my father and his goddess drift at sea,
And a boy squats on a beach in 265
Guarded by police and by relentless fate,
His eyes swimming over a dense page.

As his hero heaps the shame of the army's flight
On a crippled back, the boy begins to grasp
That never again can anyone be no one—
Unless, of course, Item 265
Turns out to be an inkblot or a fish.

Book VII Redaction

We know that Homer's Iliad is a redaction.
Robert Fagles

Under the darkening rooftree of the mind,
Twice-notched, figured with cave runes,
Generations of eyes and blistered hands
Labor over lines. In the mouth,
A faint metallic tang, iridescent
As the wings of the emperor dragonfly
Great Achilles pinched out of the air
And gnashed down. Lines of Yeats,
Of James Wright of Martins Ferry Ohio,
Lines of Catullus that once drowned my heart,
Terza Rima of Dante, Villon's welts,
And the breathless cosmic strophes of Neruda.
Lines braised on a jewel-encrusted page,
Or zigzagging like mad Odysseus' plough.
Numbers metastasizing from my list,
Spiraling down into oblique
Rhymes of cereal boxes and scripture
Of Bloomingdales, treacly cellophane
And Louisville Sluggers branded *Mantle*
In burnt umber, and the make-believe
Vapor trail from my father's paper planes.

The mind stays cowled under the moon.
The tongue is laden with metallic wings
That can't be swallowed, or if swallowed
Can't be sung. This is how it is
Without the child rocking in the house
Of his own making: sharp-edged verbs
Piercing bronze syntax, each fresh
Enjambment spurting blood, countless names
Striving under the tireless sun, foot
To spondee foot, unwilling to yield.

And this is how it must have been the morning
After the night of the burning naked girl

When Homer, dazed with longing and lost love,
Clawed open the package and his house
Went silent and his marble eyes
Swam open on a strange horizon.

The alphabet. Awkward at first—
Stuttering so the stylus could keep up.
The process—'transcription' the manual called it—
Taxed but soothed too—nothing like
Entrancement when each utterance
Dervished through his rocking torso.
No rapture with the alphabet.
His loins stayed cool, his mouth moist.
Triangles, rhomboids, circles and half-circles
Hardened into stanzas, passages.
At last, he stepped back from the workbench
And squinted at the scarred, translucent scroll.

Never before had he seen the *Iliad*.
Never realized its nuance and dimension.
Till now his version changed with every venue.
At palaces he trumpeted Agamemnon,
At sports events it was Achilles,
Weddings, Hector and Andromache,
At the titty bars the Ares bondage scene.
He'd never made it through in a single go—
That would take weeks and leave the listeners dead.
He'd never followed any blueprint.
Sure he eavesdropped on scholastic gabble—
Great gas to hear the junior geezers fret
About interpolations and mixed dialects.
Did the *Iliad* portray a bronze age—or iron?
Did 'hearing voices' mean the primitive
Corpus callosum failed as of yet to knit
Hemispheres of the pre-lapsarian brain?
Did Achilles suffer PTSD?

Did rhapsodes remember the poem
Or forget everything else?
But the alphabet began to change his mind.
No improv, no entrancement.
It was hardly verse-making at all.
An encryption, a visual echo.

Scrabbling letters Homer saw what counted
Wasn't the chant, the many-minded voice,
Not the rocking or apotheosis,
It was triumph and murder—acts of mortal men.
Not a message from another world,
Or a warped replica of this one,
With all its tedium and ambiguity.
Instead, a nape-tingling shoot-em-up.
"The world's greatest war novel."
With this newfangled Phoenician toy
Homer might give them just that.

Everything about the poem shifted—
The heroes too were cast in different light.
When he chanted they transmogrified
Into upturned faces from his audience.
There were a thousand Agamemnons,
A thousand Hectors and Diomedes.
But the alphabet defined them.
Odysseus was blunt-nosed with gray eyes
And a livid scar down his bowed leg.
Agamemnon was slim-hipped, hollow-cheeked.
Achilles' face was hooded, waves of rage
Emanated from his inscrutable brow.

The alphabet's cursives and declensions,
Its relentless absolutes and boundaries,
Its need to pluck each wave from the hissing surf,
So fixed Homer's eyes and fingers,

The poem's action veiled and he viewed the war
From a great distance. How terrible it had been
He saw now—singing viscera,
Ripped sinew and spurted black blood,
Seeing darkness flood dying eyes—
Terrible to sing a hero's death.

When deadly Diomedes hurled his spear,
And Homer's hoarse tremulo guided it
Straight between the eyes to Pandarus' nose,
The poet himself felt the tearing point,
Tasted iron blood between his teeth.
The tireless bronze sliced the poet's tongue
At the root, coming out the jaw.
Homer fell from Pandarus' chariot,
The hero-poet's armor rattling.

When Idomeneus' pitiless bronze struck
Erymas in his mouth—the divine utterance
Croaked into a shriek, piercing
The blanched skull where song seeded.
The death cloud enveloping Erymas
Closed too on the rocking, chanting bard.

How exhausting. Homer could do
One or at most two death scenes a night.
But the alphabet deadened pain, salved horror.
Carving the scenes of mayhem into code,
The poet felt a potent tingling,
His cheeks flushed as if he'd just consumed
A skin of unmixed poppy-scented wine.
Like Priam in the teichoskopia,
Homer surveyed the ornamental gore,
Far from the slaughter that had soaked his chant
And almost ruined his Osgood-Schlattered knees.
This rush that left in the belly an untouched jewel—
This must be what the sophists called 'catharsis.'

With rising excitement Homer realized
His audience would die for this catharsis.
They adored blood, loved the clash of war,
Could never get enough of his shield rattling.
Now with grisly death so telescoped,
The body-count could spike considerably.

Homer felt the gnomon's shadow lengthen,
Heard seconds dripping through the water clock.
Months passed. His beard and hair matted.
Still he bent over the alphabet,
Each morning digging deeper into the text.
Now eternity was parceled out in clauses,
Instead of brightening the rim of each instant.

Rocking and chanting he had fed the voice
And the voice had fed the utterance.
But now he could re-read, control the pace,
Compare, point, pause, revise.
Soon it became clear what had to go.
Without the antics, bells and feathers,
Slapstick was dull. The aegis too:
One thing to chant the holy words,
Another to paint them obscene on a scroll.
Still, without their presence radiating
Like a monstrance to display the underlying
Likeness of all things, the *Iliad*
Would clod-hop like that redneck Hesiod.
So in place of the holy aegis Homer invoked
The wood-nymph Simile to flit between
The eye and page. The goddess touched
His hand and his wrist flicked *suspense*
In place of *intense*, *sight* for *insight*.

In his silent office between moon and cup,
Homer's mind and eyes sharpened.

He bent close to the bleached parchment
And fancied he saw emerging from beneath
Translucent veins, arabesques and runes—
What the manual had promised: subtext.
Events subtext revealed weren't fated.
They were arranged—arising from the text.
One episode in particular enthralled.
A moment half-forgotten in the tenth year,
After Apollo's plague: Achilles' shame.
Reading and re-reading the scenes following,
The threads he first dismissed as motes of moonlight
Began to coalesce, the skein coiled.
Agamemnon's pride ignites Achilles' rage,
Swelling the high king's gall, and framing the duel
(Which he'd always played with fork and sausage)
Between Menelaus and Paris, which leads to
Hector's slagging his brother which reflects
On the braggadocious Greeks. Enter
Diomedes—a knot of skirmishes—
Back and forth doubling the movement
That preceded it and seeming
To culminate with the anti-climactic
Glaucus duel. Homer guffawed, recalling
The day he'd won the duel's rights
Dicing with an addled Corinthian bard.
A gorgeous set piece in the northern mode—
Paired patrilineal blandishments,
Comic armor-exchange and more high-jinx—
That contraption...*Deus ex machina*
To save the son of Aphrodite—poof.
Even though it came from a different era
(He never updated lingo or weaponry)
It fit neatly—presaging impending dark—
Hector's rush to the ships that sets up
Yet another confab. Then what alphabet
Manual section 18C called 'paradox':

Odysseus supplicates Achilles
Fearing Hector—who kills Patroclus,
Murdering Achilles' soul and ensuring his
(Hector's) own death, and Achilles'
At the hands of the weakest figure in the poem.
The *Iliad* wasn't sacred as it sounded,
It was engineered, symmetrical.
The gods were superfluous—a divine machine.
Yes, there was poetry throughout—
Verses descended directly from the voice:
A day of dappled seaborne clouds, or
Season of mists and mellow fruitfulness,
Or *Heart's charity's hearth's fire*,
Hundreds of lines and images unsullied
From the prime source searing the mind,
And leaving the faintest luminescence.
Who knew what future bards might glean such jewels.
But with the alphabet all that would have to go.
Along with Odysseus riddling sphinxes,
Agamemnon buying winds with his daughter's life,
Or his favorite: Thersites
Sailing in a masted penteconter
Away from Troy to distant Ethiopia.
All these scenes and poetry took place
Before Achilles chucks it in year ten.
Spectacle yes, and they delved mysteries
And revealed the character of gods and men.
But his audience cared mostly about plot.
And plot could be configured to begin
In the tenth year with Achilles' shame.
Homer could cut the rest the manual promised—
Using a technique it called 'redaction.'
Better, he'd leave them hanging—wanting more—
By cropping the poem to end with a funeral pyre—
'Foreshadowing' as the manual urged.

But for all the power of the alphabet
Spread under his hand in his silent office,
Homer couldn't swallow all the verse.
It took three thousand years to finally cleanse

The embellishments which were meant only to please the ear—stock epithets and
recurring phrases where the meaning is of no account.

Though W.H.D. Rouse did concede
To leave in the muse, for the sake of the brand name.

And when the former poet raised his beard
From the first text, the face he showed the moon
Is the face we know, ageless, marble.

Book IX Nighttown

We may be sure then that Homer had his full share of
troubles, and also that traces of these abound up and down
his work if we could only identify them. For everything
everyone does is in some measure a portrait of himself.

Samuel Butler

Passing through the outer precincts of time,
Bent with shame and longing and lost love,
Homer trods a goat path to the sea.
Sight sharpened, the former bard can
Diagram the stars, parse froth from waves,
And read the subscript between earth and sky.
But he can't compose a rocking, chanting house.
Humping a knapsack crammed with his rough drafts,
He boards a ferry from the windy coast
Across diverse waters to the bay
Where a mammoth totem of the girl who once
Had burned inside his voice holds flame aloft,
Her divine aqua monstrance signifying
Incandescence eternally unquenched,
A city brighter than any bronze tableau.

He teeters down the gangway, passport stamped
New World, and sallies wingless
Into a maze scribbled with neon,
Denizened with goddesses and fiends.
He unpockets Daedalus' cheat-sheet,
Cricks his neck to cross-check a street-sign,
Then ducks into a staircase underground.
Homer slips a coin into the slot
And hip-checks Charon's turnstile. Presently
An aegis-bearing cyclops rams the cave,
And rush hour inhales the timeless traveler.

Swaying in the vortex in between
The god of thunder and the earth shaker,
He strap-hangs with the lotus eaters,
A Yankee cap hooding marble eyes.

Time bleeds and names metastasize,
So when the monster screeches and Homer
Steps into the Queens night and gimps,
As if by memory, Jamaica streets,
And when he stamps his sandals in the vestibule
Of Homer's Famous Sports Emporium
The scriveners hardly glance up from their abstracts.
Homer's a scrivener now, though novice,
Come to Homer's for the symposium,
Here to master the art that mastered him.

Before scriveners gentrified the hood,
Homer's was Nobuddy's Bar below the El,
Where a goddess drowned Telemachus.
But now the gouged half-moons are varnished.
The brass is polished and the sheela-na-gigs
Retouched, and above the laurelled mirror
Swivel banks of plasma flat screens.

A starchy bow-tied curate nods and pulls
The thurible on a pint while Homer turns
To a gallery of glossies signed 'To Homer's'—
Achilles taunting fallen Sonny Liston,
Tarzan-costumed Odysseus swan-diving,
And Boss Steinbrenner hugging Agamemnon.
Behind him a pinky tips the shaft,
Brimming till the crown tickles the air.
The puck of glass on teak spins Homer back
To wonder at the shamrock-stamped glaze.

The symposium's upstairs. Eight sharp.
When Homer's profile breeches the threshold
The milling ebbs. All take seats
At the long table in conference room 2A—
Priam's Throne—featuring authentic
Memorabilia: treasure chest murals
And boar tusk helmet wall lamps.

Beneath the sword-blade ceiling fan
Homer finds a tuffet at the foot.

"Tonight's symposium subject is called—"
Professor Alighieri checks the page,
"The *Iliad*, I believe. A Memoir."
Fred Nietzsche's walrus stash pouts. His fingers
Furiously collate, staple, deal.
The symposiasts lean forward, chins in palms.
An instant's silence stretching for eons.

"Promising. Shows promise," chirps Al Pope,
"But such infelicitous expression."
His purpled finger taps the mimeo.
"Bowels. Black blood. Goat cheese. Knife. A tent."

Dick Lattimore mutters "Inconsistencies.
Here the ships are black, here tawny.
Did you ever actually see a ship?"

"The would-be laureate," chimes Tom Eliot,
"Evinces a weak grasp of prosody."

Simone Weil quells her strabismus
To level a fierce gaze at Tomcat.
"These women are simply forced to come and go."

"It seems," says Pub Virgilius,
From under his Red Sox batting helmet,
"The author ever favors the losing side.
Does he perhaps harbor a secret grudge?"

The victim bites his tongue. Shifts his gaze
From Chaucer's eye tic to Chris Logue's
Bronze ear wax. He's been chided.
Don't speak until the symposium is closed.

Ezra pounds the table, insists
"Kulchur *is* the work of literature.
Look how I've saxonified Divas here."
Andreas Divas pretends to disappear.
"Ezraaa," Dante drawls, "Don't hijack."

Pound slumps. The ceiling swords whir
But the heat climbs. "Dactylic hexameter
As heroic measure." "Derivative
Rhythms." "Hypotaxis." "Verasimilitude."
The workshop noses letters from the page.

"In privileging the moon and cup motif,"
Pipes in Mick Foucault, "the text subverts
Structuralist dialectic by juxtaposing
Paradigms materialist et psycho-sexual."

"Who's he when he's at home?" asks J.A.J.
He winks at Dante. "Carissimo Professore,
I feel a cloacal urge. Might we break?"

Chairs squeak, furtive glances dart,
And with a sigh the symposium adjourns.
Homer's hands tremble. His brimming eyes
Follow a finger beckoning down the stairs.
He knows now after all he's not a scrivener.
He can't make bars and squiggles translate surf.
With wobbling knees he trails behind
The granny specs and black-ribboned straw boater,
Down another flight and then another
Till they reach a door arabesqued with script.
An ashplant raps a triplet on the keyhole.

"Hold on to your hair now, Mister H," says J.
The slab swings open and he knees
The Ancient Customer forward into Nighttown.

Unearthly strobes wheel round the cosmic cave.
Eardrum-tearing bass, skank riffs explode.
In death-defying heels and rawhide collars
Brazilianed silicone sea nymphs pole dance.
Ciconean troglodytes guard the Doric arches.

"Jaysus me spondulicks!" exclaims J,
Grabbing his trousers seat. "Must have been
That cute hoor Shakespeare." His eyes
Milk the nymph tapping her riding crop.
"Mister H darlin', your pigskin please.
Propitiate Circe with some drachma."

Homer unfolds his wallet, stands the round.
He downs the crayture in a single jag.
And the next. Again. Then another.

"No bird," sings J.A.J. "A hundred wings."
Homer recalls Telemachus at Nobuddy's,
Crooning "If I had the wings of a swallow,
I would travel right over the sea."
Is this the voice's source—this amber fire?

Turning in the phantasmagorical gyre,
Homer swallows another healthy dose
And metallic wings awaken and dart up,
Figuring his skull's dissolving walls.
The space that opens is a space he knows.
The belly of a house should start to rock,
And the voice swell and the utterance vibrate.
But in this yawning cornice he hears only
The deafening back beat and crackling flame,
And his semi-nauseous rocking is untimely.

Homer gropes through chambers pulsing
With high-strung lava-flavored baubles.
His flummoxed brain, unaccompanied,

Struggles to evoke Achilles' rage,
Odysseus' madness or Atrides' pride.
He twists the dial to some far-out frequency
To tune in to the genesis of sound.
Voiceless static thrums. Silently
He numbers dactyls but runs out of fingers.

Then in a cloak of fire she appears.

If verse were conceived and spoken in one breath,
The child of distant Troy with his notched vowels
Would undulate through grottoes and owl groves.
Immersed in cascades of auburn hair,
His tongue would surf the crest of an earlobe,
Lick the aureole of a ringed nipple.
He'd rock and chant her many-tinted crown.

But all Homer has are sentences
That never move or speak. Bound in skin.
Opened only in daylight. Only alone.

Impossible to claim she is and isn't
Visible *and* deep inside his voice,
Impossible to name or even to feel
The surge of coastal nape, the crescent hip.

Slouching by Telemachus' Royal,
Or wandering a foreign windy beach,
Never had Homer seen a naked woman.
Pieces, yes, revealed, suggested,
Gliding around surreptitious glances.

But this. Encompassing, unveiled.
The lip of sea and sky blurring to clefts.
Wine cup and moon, carnal and immortal,
Consubstantiated in the chirograph
Of utterance that never was unsealed.

Maybe he could fake the pillow-talk.
Double entendres, sallies, the half-truths.
Also the furniture and bed. Even
Perhaps the legs—recumbent, pale.
But no bars and squiggles could express
The glistening ruby tympanum inverted
At the vortex of the goddess who had once
Composed a rocking house inside his voice.

Lifting his jet curls he shimmies down
Past the spangled breasts, sharp incisors
Excavating Troy 7
To the plague-ruined ribs of 7A
Deeper yet down to the navel
Silted with Priam's treasure, and the taut
Troad beneath and the archway
Between being and regression.

Long ago his father Telemachus
Had led him down a tunnel and by flare
Revealed in painted spray a horned bull's head.
"Cervix," he had pointed, "Fallopian Tubes."

But here is no depiction. His head is clasped
Between the voice's thighs. No graffiti
Could manifest this delta, this climate,
An ecosystem of dismaying breadth,
Too long for one upsweep of the tongue,
Fringed in profuse hair thinning toward
The tawny puck of deeper pungency—
A separate region, and yet borderless.

No boy examining his flesh
And flesh of other pimply boys in gym
Could ever have inferred such a landscape:
Its rasp, its vibrancy, its bruised stigma,

Its centrifugal force, its implications.
No iota accessible to pen.

Ringed fingers clutch his ears. His mouth,
Aquiver, still dumb, drips ichor.
Reaching behind she grasps his heart-
Tattooed buttocks and thrusts him into the cave
His father had once lit. Fully engulfed,
Homer plunges past runes and arabesques
Between palisades and past the portico
Into the very pith of the pergamon.
The upheaval in her ululating cry
Lasts an instant. "This is it,"
Homer thinks, thus erasing it.
"Don't screw up," he thinks, thus doing so.

Then Homer is alone on a windy beach,
Shipwrecked beneath the Pleiades and when
His eyes finally swim open he sees
His office for all the years to come:
To annotate and elegize and scrive
The distance to this echoing absence.

Still, did he glimpse, before the instant died,
A glint of granny specs? Did a tenor coo,
"Don't worry, Mister H. We'll be back."

Book XII Wiretap

I didn't know quite how to tell this story, until I realized
that if I were Homer, I'd have recognized that it isn't just the
story of men and women, but of men and women and the
gods to whom they are obedient, and told best through the
evocation of icons. So what I must do is transpose this story,
which is history, into another key, which is mythology.

—Timothy Findley

The goddess who drowned my father's heart
Was not the voice, not the girl
Who fled a burning town. The case is myth—
From cave figures to *Daily News* splash pics:
Always the Gorgon hair-do and Rilkean headline

WE MUST DIE BECAUSE WE HAVE KNOWN THEM

What the scriveners call an archetype.
And always the bronzed son-of-a-salt flatfoot
Falls for her tail and tries to get her off.
But I was there. I witnessed,
Peeking from behind a scrawny moon
The night before the summer of 265.

STONE COLD MURDER QUEEN howled tabloids.
DRY EYED WHILE CITY MOURNS DEAD TWINS

Though how would they know what grief
Sealed the Jackie O shades and silk kerchief?
That night I swooped from dreaming Ethiopia
Into the ancestral Queens row house
And saw from between banister rails flame
Lipstick smear Telemachus' neck.
I testify the queen in question sobbed.
And my father? He rocked on slippered heels
Cradling in his massive outstretched paw
A dry manhattan big as a lampshade.
At my back the bedroom held its breath.
In the cellar headphones absorbed the dark.

But heavy petting and trapeze wiretaps
Could hardly make the keystone myrmidons' case.
People's Exhibit 1: Nightclub strobes
Streaking across designer sunglasses.
2: a scarlet mouth as trashy as Fresh Kills.
And Exhibit #3 If You Please Judge,
The stone cold queen could turn to stone
Squads of suitors with a single twitch
Of her continental Lucille Clifton hips.
Who else but she would slaughter her own brood?
Truffling menstrual gore to the cave's mouth
The pigs danced wandless rooting the granite
Toe of the dolmen notching myth and time—
My Da. Detective Telemachus,
Only son of the eponymous
Hero of the first sequel,
One brogue planted in Ithaca and the other
Hooked on a brass rail in Nobuddy's Bar.

Not Circe, Sirens, and Sophia Loren
Undulating to the Macarena
Could drown my father Telemachus.

For one thing, he was already drowned.

In the summer of 265 Telemachus
Was a slab of brawn, buck-toothed, light-footed,
With a jebbie's jowls and peacock pheromones.
Being only demi-legendary
He missed Troy's sack but landed on the beach
A week after D-Day to liberate
Hittite concubines and brandy cellars.

The jacket on Telemachus has him
Pounding the wine-dark pavement to serve
Expired subpoenas on a dead-beat dad.
But that's yellow scrivening and paparazzism.

My father's only odyssey was shaking
Briskly in a Grecian urn-shaped tumbler
2 parts windy coast and 1 part Queens
And straining over rocks till the potion chilled.
Garnish with maraschino cherry bomb
And voila, he was everywhere and nowhere.

The amber goddess drowned him, coursing through
The cloudy vessels of his whale-road flesh.
She bronzed his eyes, choked his voice with wind,
And slipped into everything he touched
A mickey that kept anything from touching.

And if the pigs clamored bloody murder
It was nothing for Telemachus to turn
One Janus gob to the cave mouth
And suck her out and bind and wind
The stone queen in a skein of magnetic tape
Lubed with KY and tincture of ichor.

Cool as his manhattan Telemachus
Could transcribe and deliver to the pigs
Her stenotyped confession, notarized.

They're dead my darling twins
My singing girl and alabaster boy.
Drowned and burned my babes. Murdered them.

But leaning over the whirring tape machine,
Headphones clapped tight on waxless ears,
Telemachus caught, between sobs,
Over the static surf a strangled word.
He cranked the volume, replayed, slowed the speed
Until the utterance coalesced into a name—
As best as he made out, she said, *Thersites.*

And all that summer of love and burning cities,
As the trial proceeded under the tireless sun,
And Odysseus objected to Agamemnon,
And scriveners ejaculated headlines

QUEEN GROUNDS ETHIOPIAN AIR
MYTH TIME CHIROGRAPH UNSEALED

The goddess who didn't drown my father's heart
Dirged into his magic reel-to-real,

Thersites, rocking orphan I composed you.
And fed you the utterance and tuned you.
I made a house as if you were my child.
Why did you immolate my singing girl?
Why did you drown my alabaster boy?

And all this Telemachus typed up,
And as the summer sizzled to the nub,
His bronze gaze and tinnitus-bright ear
Converged on this one suspect *Thersites.*

In a cellar deep inside Thersites' skull
He set up surveillance, unspooled wires,
Plugged a mic into the voicebox,
Perched a spycam on the optic nerve.
And made the fist squeeze out sample jism.

Into Thersites' heart Telemachus
Insinuated his half-mythic heart,
And no matter how hard I rocked
Straining for the voice that composed a house,
I could never escape Thersites' skin.

And while Anteater raged and Floss spat
Out the aegis and Fearless chanted,
The wire kept tapping in my brain,

And the heart inside my heart coughed and choked,
And I begged my father to give the goddess up,
And I begged him not to swallow Time and Death.

All the years of white blindness till now—
The cataloging, scriving, feigning madness,
Scheming to unseat Agamemnon,
And thumbing the *Kama Sutra* with Odysseus,
Telemachus eavesdrops on my fitful sleep
Where I hear the stone cold murder queen
Mounting the pillowy stairs barefoot.

And one day soon my father Telemachus
Will corner me in my skull, make me confess
I killed the girl whose cries I could not hear,
And the boy, Fearless, my Ethiopian son.

New Poems
The Book

Compose the Simulacrum

Spinning counterclockwise into the womb,
Spirochetes hooking bits of membrane,
Flensing out of nothing density,
Flesh clotting everywhere to I.
Numbing the prime. Naming the blued swoll.
Bloody rags of thingness and damp soul.
Swards engorged from the original
Certify one exile from full null.

Every name ensorcelled in the book—
The Subway Mole, Creedmore, Vedette,
Sir Roger, Aunt Mary, the Murderess,
The Lady Prof, the Selkie, and Fearless,
The signature page aching to be born,
And every line bending to slant rhyme,
Compose the simulacrum of that spin
Figuring in counterclockwise mind
An ouroboros compassing eye and tongue—
Mortal utterance to phantom sign.
In the book, the poem's neither I nor no one.

Or, what if somehow maybe otherwise?
Drifting through the coreless universe
What if mere seed of earth and firmament
Engenders compound minds and sex organs,
Attuned to diverse rondures?

Innumerate unrecorded whispers
Slur around the counterclockwise spin
Realigning text with mortal time.
Monto, Spake, Moon, Flip, Mame,
Names absent from the book but underscoring
Every instant of six-plus decades ticking
By for you fellow traveler in hours.
A couch nap or coffee break. A browse.
And me? Beneath the orchestrated thrum

I am as you are human and I am
Each verb tiding a new is, and yet,
The tide's less real than any graven *S*.
The way I know I'm flesh is being word.

Between antinomies spins the clockwise world:
Time lived and reconceived as told.
They squiggle like an asymptotic sign.
A third's new scribed. It reckons
Its own time. Its aegis is complex
Prosody and Latinate-Hochdeutsch-Greek-
Hip-Hop-Post-Mod-Dada-Beat argot
And non-linear structure and cryptic tropes
Never conversed and unsuccessfully sung
And only painfully apprehended.
Myriad exegeses have incited
Holy wars and scholarly knife fights
And endless interpolations and edits.
This unsynced time's divorced from
(But dying to return to) the source
Within language, now outsourced.
Time, counterclockwise time distorts.
It immerses and divides maker and text,
But of the matter in the bound codex,
Ineluctable between hand and eye,
Indefatigable reader, I,
The original composer, recall
Nothing. Nada. Sweet fuckall.
The butcher paper and the rolltop desk,
The Royal typewriter and Sinsemilla smoke,
The calico cat in Berkeley and geckos
In Lubumbashi and the mice in Schull,
These, I stipulate. Doodles and porn,
White-Out and chalk dust and the aqua screen
And thirty blankety years in Youngstown—
Inquisitor, mea culpa. But these lines?
The kelson of the published book?
Memory's gone up with the pot smoke.
Maybe unlike Penelope I restitched
A different scheme each night,
And lost the thread over and over again.

Maybe I'm haunted by the orphans
Disappeared in the linguistic maze
Spinning blindfold counterclockwise.
Silenced, they utter with my mouth,
As if conceived and spoken in one breath.

But Oh It Must Be Burnt

Kim Phúc Phan Thi is the author of *Fire Road: The Napalm Girl's
Journey Through the Horrors of War to Faith, Forgiveness, & Peace*

In Flushing Queens from Camelot until
The night a napalmed girl ran screaming through
The tube to immolate the supper trays,
A boy intoned Pig-Latin Black Mass,
And slurred non-integers in algebra,
And broadcast Mets games from the toilet seat.
Afternoons on hands and knees he rocked
In front of a cabinet hi fi,
Channeling come-all-ye-diddly-eyes,
As if he could spin out from Flushing Queens,
To touch down in some phantasmagorical Erin.
Drifting to sleep, he tuned to the elsewhere,
Self-caressing, cowled in spooky aura.

In the book a simulacrum of the boy
Rocks back and forth beneath the text,
And cantillates to hex the alphabet.
Before the book there had been no before.
Every plunge backward percussed song
On bone, keying ululation.
Heels measured and the boy had learned
To quell time's surge with oceanic rhythm.

In counterclockwise omni-present tense
The codex binds heartbeat in syntax.
Colophon and sown spine and joint groove
And acid-free half-recycled leaves
And diverse narratives entrance
Eye and mind to spell all utterance.

Now the book tenses my veined hand,
Or yours, phantom reader. We are elsewhere.
Counterclockwise spins the simulacrum toward
Endless drafts blinking *save as save as,*

Past doodling through tinnitus to a place
Where there is no boy or reader only I.
And I can only channel the hi fi.

So when Kim Phúc Phan Thi
Whispers into my flight helmet, *I burn*,
America spins out of Flushing Queens
Redacting earth's aura to vapor
And decomposing human flesh to paper.
Forgive, she teaches, but I fear
Rocking elsewhere has consumed the world.

Hex

When counterclockwise hexes clockwise time
In leaves or flesh or in the simulacrum
Rocking beneath desiccated skin,
Utterance indites, words are spelled again,
Riddling augury or subversion.

Like quarks charming spacy distances,
Hex spins lust of silences,
Tense of unfired synapse, freak magnet
Between bars of the asymptotic.
Hex causes and precedes. Sans hex
Words denote. They always mean the same.
Sans hex, no leading measuring lines
Yawns dizzy to the bloody gutters,
And letters don't transmogrify to ciphers.

Hexed, every poem is a draft
Unreconciled with Nothing until passed
Deep into the phantasmagorical,
Thrumming wombward into all,
Glistening with pre-cum of the revenant.

Spinning counterclockwise hexed the boy,
Being here and elsewhere unreborn.
With billions of years and stars beyond the skein,
And billions of beings gestating inside,
I slip between to tipple, smoke, space out.
Unauthorized, the book inhales and vivifies,
Reproduces, eats, transmogrifies,
Long after I am fossilized.

Thus hexed, the meter's voiced and signed—
A mobius strip helixing an X
Chimeral with permanence. Epics
Conceived by Blank fester in a box
That unlocks only counterclockwise.
Meanwhile, corkscrewed reader, the book attests
To all that might have been sung once.

Pent

In Flushing Queens it signified constraint:
Angle, gon, gram, x, teuch.
It spelled chastity, titration, suicide drill:
Foul line, half court, far line, full court hell.
It was five boroughs I could not flee.
Five cornices of altar boy liturgy.
Five degrees of cloister. Schoolboy scansion.
Keats, Wordsworth, Milton, Tennyson.
Da DA, da DA, da DA, da DA, da DUM.

The day I overstepped from Flushing Queens
And set foot out onto the windy plains,
By thumb and Yamaha and Green Tortoise,
I first encountered sky, hashish, and Protestants,
And specimens who claimed to be poets.
How so, I asked, when they were not deceased.
Some were addled. Two saw God.
One wandered lonely as a cloud.

With the barflies and Buddhists I enrolled
In the U of D Eng Dept Graduate School,
To worship the Parnassians hired with
Spillover from DuPont napalm dash.

They'd abandoned meter—the new guard.
They evangelized shebeens and seminars.
Some absented. One tried Jesuitics.
A few guzzled themselves paralytic.
Yet all had once been pent. De Snodgrass's
Whiskers de-pented—carefully because
Of the Pulitzer ticking around his neck.
The Ohio Football Laureate had begun
"My name is James A. Wright and I was born,"
But now his lines were breaking into blossom.

The Bear pawed seminar bookshelves.
We cubs shivered under the marble busts:

Keats, Wordsworth, Milton, Tennyson.
The Bear snarled at Auden and cuffed Eliot.
We waited our turn to stand on hind legs.
We cocked our heads. We shuffled. We prayed
That this week's seminar cub would auto-de-fe
Or shit their bony ass and go feck off.

Striding over desks The Bear huffed
Pentameter was poetry's baying hound.
It baited. It was the warmonger's Johnson.
Whale Song, Turtle Mind, Prime Utterance,
Congress between Consciousness and Fur,
These, he bellowed, were the source.
Then The Bear sat, chewing a cub's ear.

;

Meanwhile off campus my Lady Greek Professor,
Moonlighting as a Sea Nymph, offered
In her water bed one foot, naked,
To my lips. Hexameter, she'd scrawled
That morning on the Aula Max blackboard,
(Bloused and skirted and in wingéd Versaces)
Sets foot upon the omphalos of the sea.
Noble and expressive, the pointer toe
I kissed under gossamer sheets daunted the hallux,
The heel waxed moony on my tongue.
The sole refracted veins of bluish light.

Homer is the first and last, she'd taught,
To gestate the sea's utterance since he is
Sole but innumerably conceived, just as
The sea froths and plumbs. In every six-
Footed line swells a wave, cresting
Over again to tongue the infinite,
Each breaking from conflict to climax.
(My ears burned with the embedded hex).
When meter lost a foot the sea recoiled,
My Sea Nymph masked as Greek Professor said,
Uncoupling word from utterance,
Leaving behind at the ocean's edge
The detritus of an asymptotic sign,
Harbinger of chirographs to come.

She twerked from podium to blackboard
And chalked a coda I could not cipher:
A perfect globe above cascading curve.
Her sea-borne breasts perked as she turned to face
The pimpled Argives in their fleet of desks.
Scanning the Aula Max, her gaze fixed
Me in the back row rapt in copying.
She peered right through as if I were a boy
Who could not rock or kiss flesh into song.

And never again from that day did I glimpse
The Greek Professor morph into Sea Nymph.

But now, as clockwise I approach the end
(But counterclockwise spinning to the womb)
That drop of ocean hovering above
The simulacrum of the ebbtide curve
Is kelson of all that I have been.
Leaping and in step; free and dependent;
It is fleetness and repose. It is the salt
wet print of the Sea Nymph's absent foot.

Vortext

; is not just sign but simulacrum.
It steps and excavates, sprints and turns
ball and heel, bridge and arch and toes.
Full revelation comes only with repose.
; is the wobble and the sole.

Something there is that doesn't love ;
Soundless; uncoupled; or else rhyming with all;
Cunning are its myriad tributaries;
Its condition speaks to injustice;
Women suffer binding, stilettoes.

When I finally stretched too tall to kiss my toes,
The flex, the curl, the spread, the sweat, the elegance,
Could not be rendered justly at distance.
I could no longer know myself, or you
Swift-footed reader, but by ;'s

Phantom nerves and tendons
Suspending ball and heel, rhyme-aslant,
Tense as air before a tropic storm,
Or buried upright terra cotta warriors.

; does not injure without cause
The lineaments of measure. No fractured
Syntax bleeds into the margin.
Conjoined otherness, unauthored and unborn
; warns and beckons simultaneous,
Totemic as an unpent ouroboros,
Livid as a tattoo on a scar.

The liminal white that binds the lunar
Necropolis to oceanic cradle is
The vortext which the perishing would cross—
But like Odysseus and Anticlea
And Jesus and his ghost personae

We cannot. Clockwise
And counter in stillness spins the vortext,
Past and present gestating the hex
In blood revenant coursing toward our nexus.

The Bear

In the time of the Sea Nymph, I sat at the foot.
Yeats's eyes were gay, but his sock was rent,
The hole redressed with a dab of chimney soot.
Because I had rocked on hands and knees for years
I knew the Sidhe and Fergus and Conchobar
And who hadn't eaten Parnell's heart.
But this was a land of cubicles and tweed.
The women were unadorned. The men, doe-eyed.

Of gyres or Noh or Kenner I knew nought.
I did not know why rhyme displeased. I did not
Know how to master the thing most prized:
Meaning. What does it mean? asked
No one ever, because everyone knew
And could explicate. I did not know who
Hunched around the table would hex, nor how
The epic with the Sea Nymph would resolve.

The Bear at the head of the oak slab seldom spoke;
With every postulation or riposte
His fur riffled and he'd grunt or sigh.
The night came when his huge paw swiped at me.
It was Monday evening, Easter 1916.
Long ago in front of the hi fi
I had rocked it with the sonorous Tom Clancy.
I knew utterance but not sign. I did not know
That ; measures stride from song to poem.

The Bear, human reader, is a simulacrum
Trundling through Galway Kinnell's poem.
Bear tracks enjamb my paperback *Body Rags*,
Criss-crossing to break meter and syntax.
Ravenous, The Bear's maw swallowed ;

It ulcerates the belly at both ends.
Between, the liminal white fractures,
Dividing dream from consequence.
Nevertheless I set off that Easter
Under the hirsuite aegis of The Bear.
To ground myself I held in thought
the Sea Nymph's divine sole against my cock.

I have met them at close of day, I rocked.
At eighteenth century houses my lips pursed
Trying to tamp the Clancy in my throat.
My tongue fluted *pahsed* to Queens *pæst*.

The fiddle rose and hovered on beauty is born.
The circle of cubs sniffed. Their ears burned.
Read straight, their eyebrows said. Don't fake a brogue.
The Bear's eyes went rheumy and he purred.

Then came two stanzas Clancy had left out.
In Queens English now, I explicated:
Padraic Pearse rode our winged horse.
Thomas MacDonagh was coming into his force,
And Major John MacBride had done bitter wrong
To Yeats's Sea Nymph the beautiful Maude Gonne.

Yeats and Homer were subjects in a book.
Pearse and Achilles were real and also not.
And true, I saw in the book what I had not heard.
The rhymes unschemed—cloud and road;
Stream, brim; horse, rider and birds
Exhaled from Being as sound-laden words.

The boy had sung and rocked as the fiddle soared
And Clancy's hi fi treble swelled to swear
Allegiance to the dream because it is
Enough to know the heroes dreamed and died.

But in that seminar air the verse was mute.
We know their dream; the Norton textbook read,
Enough/ To know they dreamed and are dead.
The table tensed. All cubs turned to The Bear.
To die, is it enough to know they dreamed?
Or does the dream cleave living from the dead?
His eyes rolled back to fur and his muzzle flared
And his forepaw swiped hard and his claw stabbed
;. The strong caesura held. Yeats trembled
No more than a stone in the living stream.

Had The Bear pierced only the toe, the dream dies.
We know their dream, only enough to know.
Had he grazed the heel, dream drowns the world.
We know their dream. And it's enough to know.

Was ; the gyre between song and verse?
Through ; could I join Bear and busts and Yeats,
And Greek Professor and Sea Nymph,
And remain the boy rocking clean of birth,
Forward into days charted by lines;
Backward like a wave or a half-rhyme;
And forward again into Easter long ago,
when my gaze first bent to read the world?

If I lost that night forever Easter's voice,
Counterclockwise I entered the vortext.

Acknowledgments

I am grateful to the editors of the following journals and anthologies, in which some of these poems first appeared.

Abraxas, Hunger's Painting; *Alembic*, Lagos; *American Literary Review*, Hoops with My Junta; Between Moon & Cup; *At Length*, Redaction; *Belfast Literary Review*, Letter to Ireland; *Poems & Their Making*, Wiretap (from *To Banquet with the Ethiopians*); *Centennial Review*, Mazembé; *Hotel Amerika*, Nighttown; *The Man of Double Deed*; *The Laurel Review*, Hindu; Scald; *New Myths/Mss*, Wiretap (from *To Prove My Blood*); *Poetry Northwest*, The Cornice of the Skull; *West Branch*, First Born; Monument; *Wild & Whirling Words* (anthology), J'accuse.

I am also grateful to the Ohio Arts Council for six Individual Artist Fellowships and the Ohio Governor's Award, to New York State for a Thayer Fellowship in the Arts, to the Ohioana Library for the Ohioana Prize, and to the Hambidge Center, Hawthornden Castle, the Headlands Center for the Arts, Fundacion Valparaiso, Millay Colony, the Ragdale Foundation, the Soros Foundation, the Tyrone Guthrie Center, Virginia Center for the Creative Arts, and Yaddo for residencies that sustained me during the writing of these works.

Publication of *The Elsewhere: New & Selected Poems & Poetics* was made possible in part by the support of Youngstown State University. Along with the support of colleagues, students, and community, the freedom to create these works been indispensable in the making of this book. For all my travels, Youngstown has been home for thirty years. What I have learned, I've tried to pass on here.

Deepest thanks to friends, colleagues, editors, and teachers who read, encouraged, and helped revise these works, including Maggie Anderson, Nin Andrews, Bruce Bond, Sheila Bucy, James Carens, David Citino, Art Clements, Bonnie Culver, Scot Danforth, William Dickey, Michelle Elvy, Elton Glaser, William Greenway, Eamon Grennan, William Heyen, Elsa Higby, H.L. Hix, Cynthia Hogue, Milton Kessler, J. Michael Lennon, John Logan, Robert Lunday, Gary McDowell, John Montague, Robert Mooney, Kevin Oderman, Steve Oristaglio, Sam Pickering, Steven Reese, Stan Rice, Jerome Rothenberg, Bruce Smith, W.D. Snodgrass, Ruth Stone, Linda Strom, Richard Tillinghast, Mark W. Van Tilburg, John Vernon, Michael Waters, and John Wheatcroft.

Special thanks to designer Lisa Reynolds, and to artist Robert Carioscia, whose images have graced my covers over the years. .

And finally, deep gratitude to Larry Moore, publisher at Broadstone Books, for his continued vision, guidance, and support.

About the Author

Philip Brady is executive director and co-founder of Etruscan Press, and a Distinguished Professor at Youngstown State University. He has taught at University College Cork in Ireland, as a Peace Corps Volunteer at the National University of Zaire, in the Semester at Sea Program, and in the Wilkes University Low-Residency MFA Program.